WE'VE GOT IT MADE IN AMERICA

★   ★   ★

WE'VE GOT IT MADE IN

A COMMON MAN'S
SALUTE TO AN
UNCOMMON COUNTRY

John Ratzenberger
and Joel Engel

CENTER
STREET®

NEW YORK   BOSTON   NASHVILLE

Center Street
Hachette Book Group USA
1271 Avenue of the Americas
New York, NY 10020

Visit our Web site at www.centerstreet.com.

Center Street is a division of Hachette Book Group USA. The Center Street name and logo are trademarks of Hachette Book Group USA.

Printed in the United States of America

First Edition: October 2006
10   9   8   7   6   5   4   3   2   1

Library of Congress Cataloging-in-Publication Data

Ratzenberger, John.
    We've got it made in America : a common man's salute to an uncommon country / John Ratzenberger and Joel Engel.—1st ed.
        p. cm.
    Summary: "A collection of essays by the former 'Cheers' star about what makes America the great nation that it is today, based on his journeys to factories and workplaces on the Travel Channel show 'John Ratzenberger's Made in America'"—Provided by the publisher.
    ISBN-13: 978-1-931722-84-1
    ISBN-10: 1-931722-84-6
    I. Engel, Joel, 1952–   II. Title.   III. Title: We have got it made in America.

PN2287.R2475A25 2006
814'.6—dc22
                                                    2006012942

To my children, Nina and James.
And to Bertha, my mother.
—J.R.

And to my wife, Fran.
—J.E.

ACKNOWLEDGMENTS

★

There are two people whom I would particularly like to acknowledge for their help in creating this book that you're now holding in your hands.

First, my editor, Christina Boys, for service above and beyond the call of editorial duty. Thanks so much for making my maiden voyage such a pleasure cruise.

Second, my agent, John Talbot. Thanks, buddy, for dropping me off at the dock.

CONTENTS

★

WE'VE GOT IT MADE IN AMERICA

★　★　★

INTRODUCTION

★　★　★

I nsofar as I have a philosophy of life, it can be explained this way: Wake up in the morning, put your hand to something useful, and take care of yourself and your family. That's it. It's simple, it's direct, and it works. And for more than two centuries that's how most people in this country lived.

I've been working steadily in the entertainment industry for more than three decades, mostly in front of, but also behind, the camera. My resumé is probably longer than Johnny Baggadonuts's rap sheet. But I can't think of a role I've ever had that pleased me more than hosting *John Ratzenberger's Made in America*. It's far from the highest-paying job, and it's the hardest one physically, given how much travel is involved and how many tasks I'm asked to do. But it's also the most rewarding job, because there are few people whose company I take more pleasure in than those who actually make things or help to make them.

By and large, America has been a country of doers, of makers, and of manufacturers who put their hands to something useful every day. We had pride in what we did and made, and produced goods that were in demand all over the world. No other explanation needed for why we—both the people who made these goods and those who owned the factories in which the goods were made—enjoyed the world's highest standard of living.

Nor was it a coincidence that one of our major exports was freedom.

Think about the fact that in 1941 Germany and Japan both had at least a decade's head start on us in terms of armaments and war materiel—everything from rifles to tanks to battleships to airplanes to ammunition. While we'd been disarming, they'd been rearming. But just like that, when necessity called, our nation retooled and turned a huge proportion of its manufacturing capacity over to the war effort. Factories that had been making lipstick holders were suddenly making shell casings. Yacht makers began supplying PT boats. And stove manufacturers pressed out armor plating.

Such examples are endless. We won the wars over there because we first won them here. Long before we were a military superpower, we were a manufacturing superpower.

What World War II signaled was that America's best days were yet to come. When our nation's factories returned to making civilian goods like cars and boats and radios, Americans produced, consumed, and exported products that transformed the American economy into an engine of prosperity never before seen in history. Not for nothing did Henry Luce call the twentieth century the "American Century."

That was the America I grew up in: mom-and-pop stores; a sense of community (and community standards); a blue-collar middle class who put their hands to something useful every day and took care of their families—and who didn't have to be millionaires to live well and happily.

My hometown was Bridgeport, Connecticut, which was in most ways Anytown, USA. That is to say, it was a manufacturing town. Bridgeport's people actually built things. Dozens of factories made chair casters and bricks and sewing machines and steel and even the little bead chains for lamps. You couldn't walk down the street without hearing the hum of an honest day's work. Our tool and die workers did their jobs believing that civilization's fate rested on one-ten-thousandth-of-an-inch tolerance. Pretty much anything you could touch or hold, somebody in Bridgeport was building it. Adults could point at something and proudly tell their kids, "I made that." And the kids understood that the widget over there didn't grow out of the earth already in its package; it was built with the help of human hands.

Which was why we learned to use our hands, too.

The only people who had it tough were repairmen—it was as if they all worked in Maytag commercials. If Dad didn't know how to fix something, a neighbor would come over to do it. Everybody had a useful hobby—like welding or boat building or radio tinkering. And everybody was happy to share their hobby with everybody else, if anybody asked. In fact, you didn't even have to ask. If Mr. Lucek found out that the Groskis needed help with their cabinets, he'd just show up and fix them for nothing. That was the essence of our community. On Saturday mornings you could see all the garage doors open, with dads and kids inside working on their pet projects, and it was wonderful.

Like America, Bridgeport was a broad mix of races and

ethnicities—Italians, Poles, Germans, Irish, Africans, Latinos, Portuguese. Yet there was no racial or ethnic tension, at least among the kids. We were bonded by the fact that our parents worked hard and, yes, made things. In school we said the Pledge of Allegiance and in summer we marched in parades on streets festooned with American flags.

Vacation to us wasn't the Catskills or Lake Champlain; it was the city park for baseball and checkers. Best of all, our Little League uniforms said "Al's Tire Repair" and "Lou's Hardware" and "O'Reilly's House of Sorrento." And you know what? That restaurant, that hardware store, and that tire shop were all kept in business by the people who worked in the factories. Those factories built more than goods. They built lives, families, and communities. Not to mention a civilization.

Well, I'm sorry to say that the America I grew up in hardly seems to exist anymore in some places. What's changed is that big-box stores are fast replacing mom-and-pop shops like the corner drug store where we used to go for sodas, and every day more factories either close down or move offshore in order to compete on prices demanded by the mass distributors before they grant shelf space.

Look no further for what's killing off the middle class in this country, working people whose jobs are dependent on everyone else's jobs. And God help us if it dies completely—or indeed, if the situation gets any worse than the coma it's in now.

Think about it this way: Everything has a cost, even lower prices. There's never going to be a factory in China that sponsors your kid's Little League team—assuming, of course, that there's still a team on that field, which there won't be if the middle class vanishes.

The exact figures about how many plants have closed down over the last decade or two aren't required to know that we have a problem—and that the problem has more personalities than Sybil did.

Anyway, I don't need statistics to know what my eyes tell me as I travel around this country for my television show, whose aim is to have a good time celebrating America's manufacturing history and excellence. What I see clearly is the damage done in communities large and small when their factories are shuttered—or when they're "repurposed," as we now say, into, among other things, outlet malls for goods made in other countries by companies that were founded in America by Americans.

Given the rate at which we're going, it's not hard to picture the day when a whole way of life will be only a quaint memory recreated in TV commercials, like that phony grandpa in overalls trying to sell phony lemonade.

Do I have any answers? Some, not all, but those that I do have are based on what appears to be an increasingly rare commodity these days: common sense. In fact, common sense (and a good memory of what used to work, as well as what didn't) is what leads me to ask these questions in the first place—questions about what we now believe as Americans, where we're heading as a country, and whether it's a place we really want to go. (Now *that's* a good question.) Come to think of it, common sense itself is usually the answer to most questions.

Frankly, I know where I want to go and where I'd like the country to go—and if the world wants in, they're welcome, too. Let everyone know that for my first act as emperor, should you choose to entrust me with that honor, I will decree that common sense be returned to its rightful place as the highest of virtues. After that, the rest is easy.

My common sense tells me that the health of our factories is a bellwether of many things, some of which have directly to do with employment and the economy and empty Little League fields; most of which have zip, zilch, nothing to do with anything connected to punching a time clock, and all of which I intend to address here.

As your emperor-in-waiting.

LIFE: A REALITY SHOW

★ ★ ★

As I write this, my television crew and I have just completed filming the third season of *John Ratzenberger's Made in America*. That means we've taken our cameras to 120 factories (and workshops) of all sizes—colossal, large, small, and dinky—and gotten to talk with hundreds of people who work in the plants, as well as the managers and owners who run them. Truly, it's a pleasure for me to do that kind of work, which doesn't seem at all like real work. Besides seeing how some great stuff gets made, I feel honored by the fact that ordinary people across the country open up to me, telling me things they'd never tell a journalist. They believe they already know me from television and sense that I'm one of them, which is true. You can take the boy out of Bridgeport, but not Bridgeport out of the boy.

I consider myself Everyman. Yes, I'm lucky enough to walk with kings when I want to, but in fact I feel more of a bond with my gardener, Ignacio, than I do with, say, the men and women who determine what we all watch, and when and where I collect a paycheck.

Why? Well, here's a true story that's typical enough for it to be labeled a defining moment. A while back I had a meeting with a high-ranking network executive to pitch a series I wanted to do that would center around life at a truck stop. The executive had been born and raised in Los Angeles, the son of a studio executive, so you can presume that he didn't lack for sophistication. But he had never heard of a truck stop—had no idea what it was. And when I explained what it was, he said excitedly, "And nobody knows about them?!"

I took a deep breath.

But I should've taken two.

Because being the son of a truck driver and the veteran of more manual-labor jobs than Jimmy Hoffa, I figured I owed it to both Dad and myself to insult him before walking out in disgust.

As soon as I got to the elevator, I knew that it had been a mistake—more, a missed opportunity. Instead of saying, "No, Dave, everybody outside area code three-ten knows what a truck stop is," I should've gently educated him by pointing out that if New York and Los Angeles were, through some calamity, to disappear one day, every other American city would shed some tears and then quickly adjust with the day-to-day work of living; but if, by some catastrophe, Los Angeles and New York were the only two remaining American cities, both would quickly shrivel and die, having lost the heart they didn't know even belonged to them.

"And that," I could've said, "is why they call it the heartland."

Too bad I didn't have the presence of mind. Frankly, it's appalling to me that a man who decides what America will be watching on the tube, thereby shaping how children and the impressionable see the world, *has never been to the United States.* The *real* United States, anyway. Too much of what he produces, markets, sells, and shows to billions around the world is, at its core, contemptuous of the country that gave him a better life than nearly 100 percent of everyone who's ever lived on this planet.

No wonder they hate us over there.

And here.

If I could, I'd grab this guy by his collar and drag him not just to truck stops, but also to factories where, sadly, fewer and fewer of the things we use every day are made. I'd force him to shake hands with the people who make those things—assuming they'd deign to shake *his* hand. And then we'd walk around the town so he could see how, in many places, factories are a town's lifeblood, and the companies themselves a kind of miner's canary. In Oaks, Pennsylvania, the Annin flag factory has been in business for more than 150 years. In Amesbury, Massachusetts, Lowell Boats has been around even longer. If either company packed up and went offshore, or closed down, the towns themselves would be sadly diminished and could even die.

That's why, on the show, I often ask management why they don't follow the trend and move. "What keeps you here?" I ask. Invariably, the answer is that the factory and community are nearly indistinguishable parts of each other.

Look at Mansfield, Ohio, where the Carousel Magic factory makes old-fashioned, hand-carved wooden horses for carousels instead of the plastic ones that, well, have no magic in them. Until about twenty years ago, Mansfield was a heavy manufacturing city, but when the plants started moving offshore, the downtown and much of the rest of Mansfield began to decay, and the cancer kept spreading. What saved Mansfield was a simple carousel—the first new one erected in America in decades that was constructed of wood, not plastic.

That seemingly simple act, which was the brainchild of a local dreamer, has had far-flung consequences. Mansfield towns-folk came by the thousands to ride this carousel that somehow represents childhood and magic and a kinder, gentler time in our history. And you didn't even have to be old enough to re-member that history to be affected by what was going on. With-out some bureaucrat social engineer coming in to decide what Mansfield needed now, the residents took care of the rest—and reinvigorated the downtown area, with vitality spreading to the rest of the city.

That's the kind of urban renewal we need all over America. We need to get back to being the industrial giant that not only won world wars, but also created thriving communities where people put their hands to something useful and took care of their families. It's not about me or anyone else returning to their childhoods. It's about returning America to its golden age.

Believe me, I didn't suddenly discover a love of manufac-turing because of my TV show. The truth is that I decided to do this show *because* of my love of manufacturing—*and* because I want to do everything in my power to make everyone aware that our factories and the people who work in them are trea-sures, our national heritage, and, God bless us, our future.

If you tune in to the show, you'll see me at my happiest. I mean, who wouldn't want to go to the Gibson guitar factory in Nashville and watch an authentic Les Paul electric being made from scratch? Or to the Airstream trailer factory in Jackson Cen-ter, Ohio? Or how about the Allen-Edmonds shoe factory in

Port Washington, Wisconsin, to see how to get soleful? Nothing better than that. Ditto the Corvette factory in Bowling Green.

The list goes on. We've visited Hartmann, Campbell's, Crayola, Zippo, Welch's, John Deere, Louisville Slugger, Steinway, Everlast, Kohler, GE, Wilson, Caterpillar, Toro, et al.—timeless, name-brand American products, rich with American know-how and American ingenuity.

But we've also visited an equal number of factories and workshops that turn out products used and heard of by far fewer people, each one no less imbued with knowledge, ingenuity, and dreams.

To watch these products come to life, and to learn how and why they're made the way they are, is a privilege—not least because the people who actually do the work take such noticeable, palpable pride in it. And at the end of the day, that's what work is supposed to be all about—knowing that what you do matters, and that you're part of something that both predated you and, thanks to your creative efforts, will survive you.

Nothing beats pride of workmanship. Nothing.

A few years ago, after my family and I moved into a new house, I asked our gardener Ignacio to dig a four-foot hole so that I could erect a pole for the flag I wanted to raise. He said he would, and in the meantime I took my kids out for the afternoon. When we got back, our backyard was home to a perfect hole—so perfect that it looked like a giant apple corer had descended from outer space, plucked out the dirt, and whisked it all away. Not a fleck had spilled on the grass surrounding this magnificent thing. It was breathtaking.

I called the kids over and gushed, "You see this hole? It was dug by a man who obviously takes pride in his work. Look at it. Fantastic, isn't it?"

They gave each other that sideways glance that means Dad's ready for the loony bin, and insisted I was making too big a deal out of nothing—literally nothing: a hole.

But it wasn't nothing. Or if it was, it was nothing in the sense that in the world in which I make a living—the world of executives who don't know truck stops from rock quarries—pride comes only with paychecks, ratings, and trophy wives, so I'd temporarily misplaced my perspective. And seeing Ignacio's job done perfectly had restored it. Which is why I have more in common with Ignacio than I do with people whose hands are callus free.

You know, moviegoers don't seem to mind sitting still for another five minutes after the feature ends to watch a list of names of people who did jobs that don't even make sense to them—jobs like gaffer and craft services and grip. Why anyone not connected to the movie industry is interested in that, I don't know. And yet, every building we walk by every day, they're all works of art that stand there in anonymity. Me, I'd like to see a credits plaque on every building that lists the names of the electricians and drywallers and roofers—everyone who worked on it. And when I buy a car, I'd like a little plate on the dash with the names of all the workers who put it together.

In other words, it's time to start honoring the people who build things—the ones who make America great and keep it free. Because when you come right down to it, it's all fine and good to be interested in which film wins Best Picture, but in the real world—which won't be here much longer if we don't care for it—it's nowhere near as important as who wins best plumber.

OUT TO LUNCH

★　★　★

On the first road trip of the first season of *John Ratzenberger's Made in America*, when the crew and I were still getting to know each other, I had one of those head-shaking experiences that feels like a life lesson even as it's happening.

We were visiting a small factory in a typical New England town—the kind of town that postcard photographers come to shoot four seasons a year. On the way there, along the main drag, I'd noticed one of those country restaurants that anyone who's ever spent time in New England—actually, any charming small town anywhere—knows from experience is going to have great food and companionship. No doubt, this was the place where locals would come to catch up with each other and scarf down home cooking that's as good, or maybe better, than what comes out of your mom's kitchen.

Finally, noon came after a long and hard morning of shooting at the factory. It was time for a delicious, restorative lunch before the rest of the day's shoot—and time to get out of there for a while. I suggested that we walk down the block to that restaurant and sample the local food and color. Good suggestion, right?

In fact, the obvious suggestion. Apparently not. My colleagues insisted to the last man and woman that they preferred to stay right there in the factory, in a windowless room segregated from the rest of the plant and workers, surrounded by cinderblock walls, eating bread and bologna brought in by the production assistant from a grocery store.

So let's recap the scene: It was lunch. We were hungry and had been working hard. A good restaurant was no more than half a block away. It wasn't raining. Nor was it cold. Indeed, the sun was blazing in a cornflower blue sky, with the temperature a pleasant seventy-five degrees. So it would've been a welcome walk.

But my colleagues preferred the misery of dry bologna sandwiches in an airless factory back room, not in order to avoid the weather or the walk or the imagined food, but, it seemed, to avoid the people. Vermonters. Otherwise ordinary folks who probably don't know box-office grosses from Nielsen ratings— which, to those for whom filmmaking is the highest aspiration, equates to pitiable retardation.

Hollywood is known as one of the most liberal places in America—presumably tolerant and open-minded. Of course, that misconception has now been debunked by everyone except most people in Hollywood. In truth, Hollywood is only tolerant of those with like-minded positions, and given how the decisions regarding what gets made and what and who get ignored are in the hands of relatively few people, that tolerant intolerance creates a de facto tyranny. The best comparison is high school, where a few cool kids set the agenda by which all the other wannabe cools have to adhere if they're to be accepted.

The difference is that in Hollywood, one's cool rating determines one's income—or, possibly, complete lack thereof. The "right" viewpoint or worldview—which in this case is usually "left"—is considered self-evident; there's little room for reasoned discussion, debate, or challenge, because in Hollywood, feelings about war and peace, homelessness and disease, and climate change and science trump facts and history.

For example, raising even the possibility that appeasement often leads to war, as it did against Hitler and, later, radical Islam, will likely get you branded as a fascist warmonger. (Bumper sticker: "War is not the answer.")

Suggesting that money, by itself, won't solve the problem of homelessness when such a high percentage of street people are there either by choice or because of addiction will earn you a "heartless" label. (Bumper sticker: "Who needs Social Security when we've got homeless shelters?")

Pointing out that AIDS in this country could be all but wiped out by the eradication of certain risky sexual behaviors (and needle sharing) makes you a homophobe. (Bumper sticker: "AIDS isn't over.")

And of course, all three of these positions make you, ipso facto, a Republican—and therefore worthy of contempt, even if your entire political worldview can be summed up by JFK's inaugural address: "Let every nation know, whether it wishes us well or ill, that we shall pay any price, bear any burden, meet any hardship, support any friend, oppose any foe, in order to assure the survival and the success of liberty."

You see, orthodoxy requires no original thought, only bumper-sticker memorization of accepted good guys and bad guys, right positions and wrong positions. If Clinton was for it, it's right. If Bush is for it, it's wrong. Even if the orthodox believers would otherwise disagree with the former and agree with the latter.

That explains why actors and writers, for example—those whose employment may be tied to personal relationships— generally keep their opinions to themselves when those opinions happen to be on the far shore of the town's mainstream. Not without justification, they worry about being specifically excluded (read: blacklisted) from work by producers and studio heads who equate conservatism with Nazism. In fact, scores of A-list people—those who determine who works and who doesn't—are on the record as loathing those whose politics they abhor. As Julia Roberts remarked before the Bush-Gore presidential election, "Republican comes in the dictionary just after reptile and just above repugnant." (She must have the concise, abridged *Webster's*. In mine, it falls between "republic" and "Republican Party.")

This line itself, which was much reported in the media, is less surprising for its politics—which are entirely predictable— than for what it says about how Hollywood views itself in the world. Here's an actress whose career and income are predicated on the public's adoration. The sole reason she can command $20 million per film is not because of her talent, per se, but because she delivers an audience of adoring moviegoers willing to plunk down eight or ten bucks to see her on that first all-important weekend. That she apparently suffered no pangs of anxiety or, later, remorse for remarks that offended the registered party of half the country—and therefore half the audience she relies on to (indirectly) pay her salary—shows that she felt insulated and inoculated, the occupant of an echo chamber in which everything she sees and hears reflects her views, and everyone she speaks with shares her opinion.

No wonder such prominent Hollywood glitterati as Susan Sarandon, Tim Robbins, Danny Glover, and Sean Penn pulled out the old "McCarthyism" card when much of the public reacted negatively to some of their cynical opinions about American foreign policy and President Bush in the run-up to the Iraq War. (Glover also voiced his support for Fidel Castro, claiming that the United States was undermining Cuba's "right to self-determination," apparently ignoring the facts—or ignorant of them—that Castro's Cuba doesn't offer free elections and executes or imprisons anyone trying to flee.)

These actors claimed that they had every right to exercise their First Amendment rights, which of course they do—but so did all the ordinary Americans who responded to their political pronouncements. Unlike most Americans, however, celebrities are able to make their opinions public because they've earned fame and therefore always have microphones and reporters available to record their thoughts, regardless of whether those thoughts are related to what made them famous. To Hollywood, the idea that free speech might come at a price doesn't compute. To Hollywood, criticism is akin to censorship—unless it's Hollywood critiquing someone else's free speech.

In 1999 the Academy of Motion Picture Arts and Sciences announced that it would present the great director Elia Kazan, who was then ninety years old, with a long-overdue honorary Oscar. Having directed such important films as *On the Waterfront, East of Eden,* and *A Streetcar Named Desire,* he was far more deserving of the award than many, if not most, of its prior recipients. But the Academy had long refused to recognize Kazan, as had the prestigious American Film Institute—better known as AFI—which two years before had flat-out refused to give him its Lifetime Achievement Award, an award, everyone agreed, he otherwise deserved.

Why? What was his crime?

Well, in the 1930s Kazan, like many fellow theater people struggling to make their way through the Depression, had believed the reports coming out of the Soviet Union in such papers as the *New York Times* (whose communism- and Stalin-admiring reporter Walter Duranty won a Pulitzer Prize for lying repeatedly about the deprivations and mass murder he saw there) and briefly joined the American Communist Party. Soon, though, he'd seen enough of Stalinism to grow not only disenchanted but also fearful of its possible impact on America through its admirers in the arts and politics. And when the (now-infamous) House Un-American Activities Committee (HUAC) held hearings about communism's reach into Hollywood, Kazan was called to testify and willingly named names of people he'd known who'd belonged to the party years before—names that, by the way, HUAC already had.

Over the years since, Kazan has said repeatedly that he didn't regret naming names. He was a patriot, born in Istanbul to Greek parents who came to America when he was a child. He had acted out of conscience, believing that Communists had indeed infiltrated Hollywood far too deeply. But for not invoking the Fifth Amendment or suffering a contempt of Congress charge, Kazan was soon considered a turncoat. And when, in time, HUAC and the McCarthy era became Hollywood's pet peeve—and was told as a story with only one side, good against evil—he became a pariah, too.

But here's the rub: Kazan would have been welcomed back into the family were it not for his stubborn refusal to apologize for his actions, as others had. Why should he? he asked, believing to his grave that he'd acted in the country's best interests. At first, when the honorary Oscar was announced, there was much talk of a boycott. In the end, there was a silent protest, with outspoken actors like Ed Harris, Holly Hunter, and Nick Nolte either sitting on their hands or crossing their arms instead of applauding.

None of those people, or the many others who'd protested either before or during the Kazan episode, presumably believes that Susan Sarandon or Danny Glover or the Dixie Chicks or anyone else who has taken some heat for their opinions about the president and the country should apologize to the people they offended. But maybe that's because Hollywood cares less about ordinary people than it cares about itself, and it can't quite grasp that the First Amendment gives you the right to make a fool of yourself but not the right to good reviews.

Personally, I long ago stopped being surprised or offended by the disparity between Hollywood's image and its reality; after all, I worked for years with some actors who are so far left they almost meet themselves circling back from the right ("The war on terrorism is terrorism," one of them once declared). But I remain ever amused by stereotypes of the other America ("flyover country," it's called) held by those who seem only to appreciate the humanity of middle Americans when they're portraying them on-screen or watching others portray them—not, as it happens, middle Americans themselves, who are less understandable to them in person than are primates in a zoo. At least the monkeys behind the bars come with a helpful explanatory plaque.

Funny thing is, these townspeople whom my colleagues back at the factory didn't want to interact with any more than they had to were New Englanders, not, say, Oklahomans; and to boot, New Englanders not from New Hampshire but from Vermont, which is, by most measures, one of the country's most liberal states.

"Really? You'd rather stay here, in this place, by yourselves, than go out and get some real food in a comfy place?" I asked them.

Yeah, they said.

As I walked off, one of the crewmen belatedly decided to join me. When he caught up, I was happy for the companionship, though I knew I would've ended up making a new friend or two anyway. At the restaurant, we took the only spare table, located in the middle, and were surrounded, it seemed, by men who for the most part dressed like dairy farmers. This was not a surprise. We were, after all, in dairy country.

As expected, the food was great. Bob, which I'll call my crewman, said he was glad he'd come, even as he leaned close and whispered how he'd kill himself if he had to live in a town like this.

Around dessert—homemade apple pie—we somehow got on the subject of September 11 and the then-new war in Iraq. Bob was vociferously against it; actually, he was against anything the president was for, even after I pointed out that Clinton's attitude toward Saddam Hussein and Iraq had been identical to President Bush's. The difference was that Bush—with September 11 in his rearview mirror—was choosing to act instead of just talk.

No matter. Bob was suffering badly from one of the first cases I'd seen of Bush Derangement Syndrome and couldn't complete a sentence without throwing in a loud F-bomb or two.

"Bush," he said. "It's all Bush. Why do you think the terrorists f---ing hate us?"

"Hey, Bob," I said, noticing others in the restaurant craning to see who the crude, rude stranger was. "You should clean up your language. That's not how people talk in public around here."

"What're you," he said, "my f---ing father?"

Ah, yes, the eternal question from those who don't like being called to account. It comes in second only to, "What're you, a cop?"

"Well," I said, "I guess you just answered your own question."

"What question?"

"About why they hate us."

"What the f--- are you talking about?"

"These people here. Right now, they're not feeling too kindly toward you."

"Well, f--- them," he said.

"Let me ask you, Bob," I said. "You ever traveled to other countries?"

"Sure."

"Europe, Mexico, the East?"

"Latin America, mostly. I love the culture there."

"So you're respectful of it."

"Sure."

"I take it, then, that you wouldn't think to go someplace in, I don't know, Ecuador and insult the locals."

Bob was cornered now, and he knew it. "You're a weird guy," he said.

"You know what's weird to me?" I said. "That you respect other countries more than you do your own. You care more about the people who want to destroy this country—*your* country—than you care about the people here. You wonder why they hate *us*. Me, I wonder why you don't hate *them*."

Bob got up and left—leaving me with the check—and we didn't say another word the final three days of that shooting trip. On our next trip, two weeks later, someone had taken his place. I should mention that it wasn't long—though it wasn't easy, either—until I found crew members who don't feel the need to don hazmat suits before meeting the general public in flyover country. Bologna sandwiches are now a thing of the past.

A HILL OF BEANS

★ ★ ★

Not far from my home is a factory that makes telescopes. A friend told me about it and suggested a quick tour to see whether it might make a good *Made in America* segment. On the way there, I heard some incredibly depressing news on the car radio: Ford had announced plans to lay off a full quarter of its workforce—more than twenty-five thousand people—and shut down fourteen plants.

The news report ended with what I believe had to be the quotation of the year, from Ford chairman Bill Ford. It left me shaking my head but understanding what had happened to this company. "From now on," Mr. Ford said, "our products will be designed and built to satisfy the customer, not just to fill a factory."

Well excuse me, but shouldn't that have been obvious for about, oh, I don't know, fifty years? The fact that the chairman of one of the three largest auto makers in the world issued that statement on the day he publicized the most severe economic medicine in the company's history is truly remarkable. But it confirmed what I already knew about too many established businesses: that after they got where they were going, they forgot what got them there, so they couldn't keep going further. (General Motors, by the way, had fallen into the same business quicksand, as their reported results of a few days later would confirm: a quarterly loss of nearly $5 billion—that's billion with a "b"—as well as layoffs and plant closures.)

All companies, no matter how gargantuan, began with an idea for a good or a service. And the idea probably took shape in a garage—metaphorically, if not actually. That is, the company that was formed to bring the idea to the market was brainstormed and fretted over and defined and refined and shaped and whatever other verbs were necessary to reach fruition. Maybe at first the whole company was just that person who'd had the idea, the one with a vision and guts. But eventually others joined, the public voted with their pocketbooks, the business grew, and the rest became history.

Unfortunately, history also shows that companies that succeed—especially as wildly as Henry Ford's Ford Motor Company did—often lose their bearings as the second and third and subsequent generations take over. By then the corporation has become a kind of living, breathing organism whose purpose, like that of all living organisms, is to stay living. It has to survive, and survival—for the sake of everyone who works there, particularly the decision makers—invites caution. And caution invites accountants.

You know, bean counters. Corporate bean counters.

I'm not much for the derisive nicknames that sometimes accompany jobs—like "suits" to designate the bosses as opposed to the "talent" (which, come to think of it, isn't a term I like any better). Even so, "bean counters" is an apt way to describe the people who now seem to be disproportionately heading major companies. They count beans coming in and beans going out without obvious regard for much beyond keeping more beans coming in and fewer beans going out. That doesn't leave much room for anything that isn't quantifiable in the bean ledger, like vision and guts.

At first, the strategy works—but only in the way that a car that has labored to reach the top of a steep hill can coast in neutral until it hits the bottom on the other side and meets the next hill. The momentum will eventually be gone. Then what? Well, if bean counters are behind the wheel, they won't really understand that stepping on the gas requires a return to what made the company great in the first place. They're incapable of seeing anything other than cash inflows and outflows.

You notice the same dynamic in dozens of industries, but it's interesting that two of them that disproportionately affect the general public should find themselves in similar troubles at the exact same time: cars and Hollywood.

Much has been made these last few years of Hollywood's box-office troubles. At first the "experts" laid it off on the almost-vertical increase in DVD sales. Conventional wisdom said that people were content to stay home with the family, eat their own popcorn, and watch a DVD of whatever was available. This was, proclaimed the experts, the home-entertainment revolution. Then, unexpectedly, DVD sales flattened. But instead of people returning to the multiplex, even fewer of us showed up. So now conventional wisdom pointed to the high cost of movie tickets and theater popcorn (which, by the way, is a beef that dates back at least to Shakespeare's time, so we're five hundred years and counting on the high cost of entertainment and grub).

The real reason even people who love movies are staying away from movies is that there are so few movies to love.

That's what happens when the suits and bean counters are in charge of the process. You get movies that were made as if on some assembly line; they're considered products that have been focus tested by people who know the price of everything but the value of nothing, according to whether they have the right "elements" attached—an element being a script, a director, a star or stars. What happens too often, though, is that the script becomes the least important element, and the names attached (Tom Cruise, for example) become disproportionately important. It's believed in Hollywood's upper echelons that moviegoers will pay on that all-important first weekend to see "the new Tom Cruise film" regardless of how good it is, or how plausible, or how entertaining—which is why Tom Cruise gets paid $25 million; the man consistently brings an audience. But the truth is that you can put Tom Cruise and Julia Roberts and Denzel Washington and every other colossal star in a film that ends up losing money. Why? Because although it did great that first weekend, when the stars' devoted audiences showed up, by the following weekend word has gotten out that the movie, despite its star presence, isn't worth seeing. So the rest of the audience that's hungry for a good film stays away. For them, it's not enough to have the "right" talent attached; for them, the whole movie has to be good.

Now come the postmortems and finger pointing—the marketing was bad, the stars didn't promote it enough, the release date was wrong, the advertising campaign stunk, and so on. Though there may be truth to some of it, it's all beside the point when the movie should never have been made.

Thirty years ago a relatively unknown actor named Sylvester Stallone tried selling a script he'd written about a down-and-out boxer who lucks into an improbable chance at the heavyweight championship. It was a terrific script, and everyone who read it thought it could be a big hit—as long as some big star like Robert Redford took the title role. You see, the conventional wisdom—even in the mid 1970s, a great era in American cinema when excellent movies came out almost every month—was that boxing movies were dogs at the box office. The only way to get them made was with stars that the studios presumed people would pay to see, regardless of the subject matter. The problem here was that Stallone insisted on playing the boxer. Universal pleaded with him, offering more money for the script than he'd ever seen in his life. But instead of taking the money, he risked everything and held firm. He believed in his product and in himself, and that passion guided his instincts—despite his being about five foot eight and 165 pounds, more like a middleweight than a heavyweight. In the end, Universal decided to make the film anyway, but instead of a relatively lavish budget, it spent only a million bucks on this boxing movie with an undersized unknown lead. That way, if no one came to see it, the whack wouldn't be too bad. Well, as it turned out, *Rocky* earned almost $225 million (about $775 million in today's terms) at the box office as well as the Academy Award for Best Picture.

So what's the moral? Well, the moral for most normal people is that moviegoers, above all, like a good story. But for the powers that be in Hollywood, the moral was that boxing movies were hot. I'm not kidding.

Suddenly, Hollywood decided to order several boxing movies, expecting that same kind of magic at the box office that *Rocky* had created—so of course there soon followed some boxing movies (like *The Greatest*) that were terrible and tanked with the public. Now, did they tank because they were boxing movies? Of course not. They tanked because they weren't good movies. Fast forward to 2004, when Clint Eastwood wanted to make *Million Dollar Baby.* Warner Brothers couldn't see the emotionally powerful story, only its boxing backdrop, and passed on the chance to make it, explaining that boxing movies weren't commercial. So Clint took the script elsewhere and the movie he made earned a ton of dough and won the Academy Award.

The most essential fact of movie making is this: You can make a bad film out of a good script, but you cannot make a good film out of a bad script regardless of how good the actors, the director, the editor, and the cinematographer are. And if there's a single overriding reason these days that fewer and fewer of us are showing up to buy movie tickets, it's because less time is spent on scripts—making the stories as good and as tight as they can possibly be—and more on everything else. If the right actors and director are in place, a movie will get made even if the script could use another draft or three to work out the kinks—or even if no number of drafts could work them out.

The one consistently happy exception I can think of is Pixar, the animation studio that gave us *Toy Story, A Bug's Life, Finding Nemo, The Incredibles,* and *Cars.* I can tell you from personal experience, as—I'm proud to say—the only voice actor to have appeared in every Pixar-made film so far, that the whole Pixar team is utterly and entirely devoted to getting it right on the page before they start putting it on the screen, sometimes taking two years for writing and rewriting. No wonder. John Lasseter, Pixar's creative chief, is a man of vision and guts who encourages passion for the work from everyone there. And his boss will settle for nothing less. That would be Steven Jobs, co-founder of Apple Computer and one of the modern world's true visionaries. Steve may not be able to draw a straight line himself, but he understands and appreciates better than anyone what creative people can do when you demand excellence and allow them to do what they can. Every frame of every film Pixar makes reflects that, and their excellence is rewarded at the box office. Pixar films are always major hits. The whole family can enjoy them, with kids laughing on one level and their parents appreciating another level of wholesome sophistication that is rare in these days of screen cynicism.

That's why it was such good news when Disney bought Pixar (coincidentally, a day after Ford's dire announcements) and installed John Lasseter as its animation studios' chief creative officer—meaning that Pixar's philosophy is once again Disney's philosophy, the one by which Walt Disney lived his life and work. I have to believe that the day of the acquisition was the day he stopped spinning in his grave, which he'd been doing for years, since the company that he'd founded stopped trusting the creators of great entertainment and began listening more to people who advocate this way: "Let's see, *Treasure Island* is a classic work of literature that we did okay with fifty years ago in live action, so why don't we make an animated movie of it—except, yeah, I know, we'll put it in outer space. That's right, we'll call it *Treasure Planet*. Perfect! Now, what's it about?" Working by committee and focus groups, they'd gotten safe and complacent, lacking all the passion that had driven Walt to risk everything on this studio in the first place.

My personal association with Pixar is a function of my complete admiration for the company, but I also have enormous affection and respect for a number of companies that I know only from touring them on my TV show—companies that I could see as soon as I walked in the door were built on vision and guts, and sustained by passion. A bagpipe company outside of Cleveland makes some of the best bagpipes in the world, because the Scottish emigrant founder will settle for nothing less. A luggage company in Southern California can't keep up with demand for its expensive goods because the founder demands perfection, and that takes time. A shoe company in the Midwest was founded by a man who believed that shoes ought to be comfortable the moment you first put them on rather than after a few blistery weeks.

There are dozens, hundreds, thousands of examples of successful companies started by people who built better mousetraps. That's the DNA of moxie, of success, on which America was founded, and it's why so many other countries always seem to hate us: they reflect old and calcified cultures struggling to hold on to past glories without taking the steps necessary to assert themselves—sort of like Ford and GM, I guess you could say.

England is better than most European countries, but when I lived there for ten years, I learned the hard way not to let anyone know that I was going to take a vacation in Malta, or make a film in, say, India (*Gandhi*), or buy a new car, even if it was used. "Oh," my neighbors would say, "Mr. High and Mighty. Well aren't you the one?"

Meanwhile this country, the upstart, the first ever to be founded on an ideal by risk takers with vision and guts, is the only country where people consistently applaud, congratulate, and encourage success. Sure, there are always a few here who feel that the only way they can be as tall as you is to pull you down to their level with insults and sour grapes, but as a rule we beat a path to the doors of better mousetrap makers.

Which is why it was so distressing to hear Ford's chairman—a member of the family himself, a direct descendant of founder Henry—admit that they'd all forgotten what had once made this great company great.

When I got to the telescope company for my impromptu tour, I asked the founder whether he'd heard the news about Ford.

"Yeah," he said, "it's a sad day for everyone, but I think something good will come of this."

We talked for a while about what we all could learn from Ford's and GM's mistakes, and then it was time to get to the business at hand. "What," I asked, "is the most important thing about making great telescopes?"

"Not to be nearsighted," he said.

~~SEVEN~~ SIX LESSONS
I'VE LEARNED (SO FAR)

★　★　★

I'm a fast learner. Except for when I'm not. But over the past three seasons of visiting factories I think I've observed enough, and absorbed enough, to share some salient lessons with the world—lessons that would seem to translate to other businesses as well, if not life in general.

First, I've learned that when the president of the company—*the president*—calls me "Cliff," it's going to be a long day. A long, long day. And that we're not going to get along all that well.

Second, I can state categorically that the smaller the company, the better the lunch I'll be served. Serving our crew lunch during the long day of shooting is a custom observed by most companies we visit, from Fortune 50s to five-man workshops. But serving us a delicious lunch as opposed to something that's just edible is a custom observed only by the companies that one would think can least afford it. Without question, the five-man workshops put out the best spread. I remember the time we were at one of America's most famous companies—a corporation that makes products that every one of us uses every day of the week. And you know what they gave us for lunch? Change for the vending machines . . . four flights down.

A few days later, though, we found ourselves in a factory that makes a niche product with such limited appeal, I doubt most people have ever touched the thing. But the owner of this factory—well, you can't really even call it a factory; it was more like a garage—laid out a king's feast for me and my guys. There was so much food, we skipped dinner that night and had only a light breakfast the next morning

So what's the lesson? Well, I'm sure you can infer your own, but I'll tell you what I think, because the example isn't isolated, nor is it confined to something as unimportant as food: Across the board, the smaller the company, the better the hospitality. Which tells me that the more likely a customer or a client is to come in contact with the CEO, even if only by accident, the more responsive the company will be to that customer's or client's needs. And that means that the more insulated the top brass is from the people down on the factory floor, the more impersonal the working experience is going to be. Without question, it's a much different feeling being shown around a factory by the guy who built it than by the person who got the job three generations later—just as there's a difference between taking a tour of your best friend's new house and walking around some historic castle while listening to a recorded guide. The issue is ownership and responsibility.

Ownership is a human-nature issue that extrapolates into almost every avenue of life. For example, once upon a time someone who was down on his luck got help directly from the people who wanted to help him—like church members. Real live human beings handed that person money, or food, or clothes, or whatever it was he needed, so that person felt connected to his benefactors. He felt grateful. And obliged to them. So he did whatever he could to get out of his bad situation as fast as possible, and he likely also wanted to lift himself into a position where he could, in turn, help someone else the way he'd been helped. That dynamic was good for him and good for those who helped him. Close proximity between giver and receiver created a sense of investment on the part of the giver and a feeling of obligation in the receiver. That helped to keep the social and emotional fabric of the country strong.

But when the government elbowed itself into the scenario and welfare graduated into entitlement, America ended up with an impersonal system that failed all of us—the taxpayers whose money was being sent to faceless names, and the recipients who had only to mosey down to their mailboxes every month in order to "earn" their money. Gone completely was the incentive to get off the dole created by face-to-face contact. And boy, when that check was sometimes a day or two late, watch out. Hell had no fury like a deadbeat when his "paycheck" was delayed.

Anyway, this isn't about welfare; it's about ownership and responsibility and customer service and communities where you don't honk at the slow driver in front of you because it might be your neighbor's Aunt Ida. It's about stores where everybody knows your name—or used to. It's worth thinking about these lessons, because if a TV crew that's going to be giving a company millions of dollars worth of free advertising can't get a plate of something hot and tasty for lunch, then you have to wonder how an ordinary customer just off the street is being treated. And by the way, that applies whether it's a factory or a store.

Which brings me to lesson number three: I've learned that when a company's publicist doesn't work directly for the company, there's bound to be some major disconnect between what the publicist told us we're going to see at the factory and what we actually *do* see. According to my complex calculations, the amount of that disconnect is proportional to the distance between the publicist's office and the company's factory or factories. This, it would seem to me, is a corollary to the welfare syndrome, in that publicists who work far away rarely have any real feel for the company's products. The company is just another client to them, which obviously means they can't have any feel for the people who work in the plant, which is where the connection comes in. In my experience, the best thing a third-party publicist can do for me and my producers and crew is to introduce me to the plant manager and then get out of the way.

That leads me to my fourth lesson: I've observed that the more the company brass knows about their employees, the happier that factory floor is going to be. Now, of course, that doesn't mean the chairman of GM needs to know that the guy welding chassis at station two on the Pontiac Grand Am line is named Bob, and that he has a wife, two kids, and loves snowboarding, pizza, and Vin Diesel movies. Clearly that doesn't make any sense.

But I do believe that someone who has a direct line to the executive suite should know that sort of stuff about each employee—not necessarily because it's polite, but because it would seem to be good business.

By now I know how to read a factory's mood when I walk in. It's actually not too complicated. If I see smiling faces, that's a good sign. Frowns—a bad sign. And if I see employees who're proud of what they're making—like the guy who shouted out to me, "Best damn conveyor belts in the world!" at the conveyor belt factory, even when the cameras were off—I know that this is a good place.

The more pleasant places are naturally the most congenial places, and the most congenial places appear to be the most dynamic places—and the most dynamic places are invariably the ones where the man who takes me around the plant knows everyone by name and can tell you what schools their kids go to.

Conversely, the least congenial factories seem to be the least productive. Those are the factories where workers are more likely to sidle up to me and whisper complaints that they feel unappreciated, like they're unimportant to the company. And guess what? More often than not, when I hear things like that, it turns out that the factory's ownership is located far away.

I remember one plant we went into where the employees would do this: "Psst, over here," like they were trying to sell me stolen watches in the alley. And when I got there, they'd talk about how this place had really changed and gone downhill since old man Bishop died and his sons sold out to the big corporation.

Well, I didn't have to be told that to already know it. It was something I'd just felt the minute I walked in that door in Ohio—and met the publicist . . . from New York.

I remember another plant where there were signs on the machines saying, "This machine has no brains, so use yours."

How incredibly insulting is that? The signs could just as easily have said, "Be careful." But management, who answered to headquarters a thousand miles away, had phrased the safety message in a demeaning way. Not intentionally, maybe; and in fact, I bet it was completely inadvertent. But that just proves how out of touch they were with their people, not to know that the message would be seen as a big upraised middle finger.

I whispered to one of the ladies on the factory floor, "What do you think of these?" and she said, "Oh, we hate them, but what can we do?"

Well, maybe *she* couldn't do anything, but I could. I did what the workers would've been fired for doing. I walked around like Norma Rae and pulled the signs off each machine. People cheered me. Even if it was just for that one afternoon, morale was raised—and, I have to believe, so was productivity.

True, when we bring our cameras into a plant, no company is obliged to open up its books to us. Still, it's plain common sense that workers are happier when they're acknowledged and valued as human beings who have real lives; and that a happy workforce is a productive workforce; and that a productive workforce brings greater profits to the company.

My fifth lesson is this: I have discovered that watching cheese being made is a surefire cure for two things: insomnia . . . and a love of cheese.

There's nothing I can say on the subject that the great G. K. Chesterton didn't already say better when he dryly noted, "Poets have been mysteriously silent on the subject of cheese."

No wonder. Cheese making is like watching grass grow. For goodness sake, it's cheese. It's not a sports car or an airplane, or even a fishing rod. It's milk that goes bad. Plus, they wanted me to wear one of those hairnets, which to me is a deal breaker.

The final lesson I've learned so far is the most important: America's factories are its heart and soul. In smaller towns, they're frequently the de facto crossroads of the community. And in larger cities, they become de facto small towns—communities unto themselves. Which means that, together, we have to do whatever it takes to keep them alive and operating at full capacity so that we can keep the American dream alive for another generation.

It's great to be a rock star, flailing around the stage and cashing huge checks and picking out the groupies lined up at your door. But somebody has to get up at six-thirty every morning, even if he's hung over, and go make that rock star's guitar at the guitar factory. In fact, somebody has to make the loudspeakers and amplifiers and the stage, and somebody has to make and drive the trucks that carry all that equipment from one place to the next. Somebody has to make every single item that all of us use every day.

All of us, we are part of the same show, so we're only as strong as the weakest link. Which means that we're all responsible for strengthening whatever that link happens to be at any given time. And then when that's fixed, we move to the next weakest link, then the next one, and so on, and so on. Forever. Since there's always going to be a weakest link.

That's really the only lesson anyone ever has to remember.

THEY DON'T MAKE 'EM LIKE
THAT ANYMORE

★ ★ ★

We were driving across Pennsylvania, heading for a factory in western New York, when we stopped for lunch at a truck stop. One of the truckers recognized me and said he watched and liked the show, and lamented how much better he'd feel if the shoes that accounted for most of his lading had been made in America instead of being shipped from China.

"It kills me, you know," he said. "I can't remember the last time I loaded any shoes made here. I kinda feel like a traitor, if you know what I mean." His big, beefy hands thumped on the counter as though he were nervous.

"Well," I said, "the solution isn't for you to stop trucking. It's for Americans to start making more shoes."

"Amen to that."

Then someone else who'd overheard our conversation joined in. His name was Lewis. His craggy face told me that he was up there in years, but his shoulders weren't sloped, and I could tell that if he stood, he'd still be well over six feet. He said that, as a matter of fact, this whole area in and around

Binghamton used to be one of the country's leading producers of shoes.

Lewis was a local who'd retired years before from whatever it was he did (he didn't say). He'd grown up there in the 1920s, he said, and described the town before the Second World War as a haven for white European ethnics—Poles, Russians, Czechs, Ukranians, etc.—who'd come in search of work in numerous factories, especially those making shoes.

"And they came," Lewis said, "because of one man—George F. Johnson."

I'd never heard of George F. Johnson, but after listening to Lewis—and then confirming what he told me—I'll never forget him. His biography should be required reading for anyone who owns a manufacturing company, especially one that's contemplating a move overseas in order to cut costs.

In 1870, Johnson left school at age thirteen to work in a boot factory in his hometown of Milford, Massachusetts. It was a business that apparently agreed with him. Full of ideas and plans, he soon moved to Binghamton for a job at the Lester Brothers boot factory, which he'd heard was a place that welcomed ambitious young men like him. Turns out, he'd heard right. And in 1884 he convinced his employer, Henry Endicott, to build a new factory outside the Binghamton city limits in what became known as Lestershire. At the time and for obvious reasons, it was considered a radical notion to locate large factories away from the city's crowding and congestion. How were the workers to get there? Well, get there they did, in spite of the difficulty.

A few years later Endicott promoted Johnson to production and sales manager, and a few years after that he sold him a half interest in Lestershire Manufacturing Company. It was now the turn of the twentieth century, and times were lean for several industries, including shoes. A shakeout had left Lestershire still standing, but barely. Johnson, however, had the prescription: cut out frills and unnecessary costs, and give the workers incentives to produce by paying them on a piecework basis at a good rate. The harder they worked, the more money they made.

Bingo.

Within two years the partners formed the Endicott-Johnson Company and, in a village west of Binghamton, built a leather tannery that would soon be incorporated as Endicott. Joining E.J., as it was generally called, to the old Lestershire Company created one of the largest shoe manufacturers in the Northeast.

By the time Johnson became president of E.J. in 1920, he'd implemented his plan of providing workers with quality homes, built by his company, at affordable prices on reasonable terms. Many of the homes—solid and unadorned but better than today's basic tract models—are still standing and sell for prices that would amuse Johnson, who could've lived anywhere but chose to live with his family in one of them, among his workers . . . with whom he also socialized . . . and for whom he'd established a profit-sharing plan.

No wonder Lestershire incorporated as Johnson City.

It was the way Johnson treated employees that accounted for why Endicott-Johnson did so well, soon becoming the largest manufacturer of shoes in the whole country. He wanted his people to be happy and healthy, because he knew that happy, healthy workers make better products, and make those products faster. The term for the kind of capitalism he practiced was called "benevolent paternalism."

Johnson paid for his employees' medical care, not just

insurance, and handed out shoes to all of his employees' children every Christmas. He gave banquets and parties, all free, and built libraries and recreation centers and parks, with free boating and swimming privileges. The George F. Johnson Pavilion, erected during the Depression, attracted famous-name big bands. For a buck, the people of Binghamton could dance all night to Tommy Dorsey's band, featuring Frank Sinatra. And to this day, Binghamton boasts the largest collection of operating merry-go-rounds of any city in the world—six of them—all donated by Johnson, who never charged anyone a cent for a ride.

Both Johnson's and the company's reputation grew internationally. Immigrants would land at Ellis Island not knowing a word of English, with hand-drawn signs hanging from their necks: "Which way, E.J.?" Friendly customs and outreach workers would make certain to get them on the proper train to Binghamton, where old George F. put them to work. And work they did. At its peak, Johnson employed about twenty-five thousand people and turned out almost two hundred thousand pairs of shoes *a day*, all made by hand. During the Depression, everyone tightened their belts a little, but Johnson never laid off a single worker.

George Johnson died in the mid-'50s, both happy and wealthy. Alas, his factories mostly sit idle today, our shoes now made almost anywhere but here, as my new trucker friend's haul bore out.

"They don't make 'em like that anymore," said Lewis.

"What?" I said. "Shoes or people?"

"Both."

"Hell," said the trucker, "even if someone wanted to do business like that, the lawyers wouldn't let 'em."

True enough, I said, imagining some lawyer nipping at the heels of any boss who wanted to provide free health care to his employees, claiming the potential of a lawsuit in which the doc was accused of giving substandard care, or that the policy denied the employee some invented civil right. And even if the boss got past that, there'd still be so much red tape to work through and so many governmental agencies having to approve every perk, he'd go out of business because he'd have to spend all his time trying to comply with the law.

"Well," said the trucker, needing to hit the road again, "we'll not see his like again."

"To George F.," I said, raising my mug of tea.

"To George F.," they said.

Back in the RV, I slipped off my shoes to see where they'd been made, expecting to read "China" and preparing to toss them out. But they didn't. They were Allen-Edmonds, made in good old America, one of the few.

Which is why, the following season, we brought our cameras to Port Washington, Wisconsin, where they're made.

THINKING OUTSIDE THE BIG BOX

★　★　★

Before I was lucky enough to make my living on the stage, I worked some very tough jobs—enough to value the meaning of hard work. Crewing on an oyster boat, for example, is something everybody ought to have to do for a while, just the way we used to compel military service. It'll make a man out of you real fast—an old man. I recall that first morning—4:47, to be exact—standing excitedly on the dock just as the sun was about to crest on the horizon. I stood there remembering the great sea-adventure books I'd read by Melville and Conrad, imagining myself as one of their romantic characters. Then, as I stepped on deck for the first time and heard my boots on the wood, I knew that this was exactly what I'd signed up for. Having grown up across the street from the Atlantic, I'd heard a thousand tales, some even true, from those salty dogs who had spent their lives defying the watery frontier. Now, at last, I was one of them. We cast off and set out.

The next thing I remember, but just barely, was not having the energy that night to stand long enough to get undressed. My fingers didn't even have whatever it took to unbutton a shirt. That single day had been six weeks of boot camp compressed into nine hours—or what felt like nine hundred hours. I woke the next morning with only enough time, and energy, to brush my teeth before reporting back to the ship. For the rest of that incredibly long day, every waking—or what passed for waking—minute these words played over and over in my brain as if on a continuous loop: *What the hell were you thinking?* Dredging for oysters in steel nets, and raising them and lowering them, putting them in a metal sleeve, separating them by smashing them with steel bars, loading oyster bags—that's only some of what has to be done, and there's never a down minute. Believe me, you do that work for even a couple of days, you'll never again complain about having to carry pianos up five flights—which was more or less another job I had.

Cross my heart, I'm glad that I no longer need to work as hard as my dad did all his life; Mom, too. Which is to say, I don't romanticize hard work. Hard work is hard work; it's hard on your hands, on your back, and sometimes on your spirit. But even so, it's ultimately ennobling, no matter how menial it may be, if the job is done well. As the theater adage goes, "There are no small roles, only small actors." The truth is, what built America and what always kept America strong and free was that famous Protestant work ethic that you didn't have to be Protestant to follow.

For my television show, I have to travel an enormous amount. We visit literally every part of the lower 48, from small towns to big cities. So when I say that I fear America is hemorrhaging, it's not just a feeling I get from reading the *New York Times* or the *Seattle Post-Intelligencer* or the *Chicago Tribune*, or from watching CNN. It's from going into factories and talking to the people who work in them. Workers who believe in the value of hard work and the confidence-building satisfaction of a job well done. These are the people who fear the day that their own place of business moves offshore and they, too, lose their jobs like the millions before them.

I promise you, I've either read or heard most of the arguments for and against Wal-Mart, and for and against NAFTA, and for and against protectionism. It's not an easy issue, nor is it easily defined with good guys and bad guys. Manufacturers are in a game of survival. To stay alive from day to day, they have to sell their wares to major retailers who insist on acceptable quality products at prices that may be impossible to achieve without major concessions, usually to geography. China has a billion people and they all need work, even if it is for pennies an hour—which is more or less a living wage there (while here we don't even bother to pick up pennies off the sidewalk). Plus, the Chinese are reasonably educated, relentlessly hard-working, and utterly dogged. As a nation determined to make the twenty-first century the Chinese Century, just as the twentieth century was the American Century, they have the motive, the means, the opportunity, and the real estate to build factories to any specs American engineers can devise. And they don't have trade unions or collective-bargaining contracts. When American manufacturers see what it costs—rather, *how little* it costs—to build their doohickeys and thingamajigs over there, they face a colossal dilemma.

What are they to do? Well, if their major competitors are doing business offshore, and they're beginning to lose market share and their shareholders are screaming for better earnings, they really have little choice but to go where they can compete better and more efficiently.

Meanwhile, we all blithely park our foreign cars in the big-box store's parking lot, which occupies the spot where a dozen smaller stores used to be, and go inside to buy American name-brand products that used to be made two counties over but now come from fourteen time zones away. Why? Because you can't beat the prices. And that's a powerful, maybe irresistible, lure. One study I read, from a legitimate economic consulting group called Global Insight, said that Wal-Mart's low prices increase Americans' purchasing power about $120 billion a year, which works out to about $400 per person. And that's in hard goods. In groceries, the savings may be even more important. Wal-Mart's ridiculously low prices are as much as 40 percent below regular supermarkets. So because the poorest Americans spend a far higher percentage of their overall income on food than the affluent do, by shopping at Wal-Mart they can stretch their food budget by 20 percent. There's no denying the great good that Wal-Mart and Costco and the other big-box stores do. But like everything in life, that good comes at a cost. To offer such low prices at retail, the stores have to buy wholesale at prices that, more often than not it seems, preclude manufacturers from manufacturing those goods here.

It is one of the great ironies of our time that the man who's arguably responsible for this turn of events believed strongly in selling American-made goods, and in fact titled his autobiography *Made in America*. When Sam Walton, Wal-Mart's founder, was in his prime and his new but fast-growing store chain was located only in small towns, he used to insist that, whenever possible, the products on his shelves bear that "Made in America" sticker. And he publicly shared other Americans' concerns when, in the late 1970s, our country began to experience a severe trade deficit, primarily with Asia. Lost dollars translated to lost jobs, he declared, pointing out in 1985 that 1.6 million American jobs, mostly in manufacturing, had been eliminated in the previous four years. His response was to implement a "Buy America" campaign at his Wal-Mart stores. It was a good idea, but by then it had limits. Americans used to spending less were of no mind to pay more, so that put Wal-Mart at a competitive disadvantage against other retailers who knew that as long as the item cost less, their customers—us!—wouldn't care that the tag said "Made in China" as opposed to "Made in America." Even before Sam Walton died in 1992, Wal-Mart's shelves were mostly filled with goods that were once made in this country but now came almost exclusively from offshore. Why? Because that's the way we the people want it. Almost every retail survey confirms that the number one factor in where we buy an item is price. No wonder Internet sales are exploding. Someday there may be only a handful of brick and mortar stores left—Wal-Marts and Costcos.

In a way, we're like the heroin junkie who buys from the pusher who buys from the middleman who buys from the smuggler who buys from the processor who buys from the grower. There are eleven thousand miles between the hypodermic filled with smack and the poppy fields where it all began, but it's a short line of cause and effect. Our appetite for low prices is what keeps those Chinese factories humming.

So we cannot, and should not, pretend that our affection for big-box stores hasn't changed our whole way of life. These stores—in fact, mass merchants in general—have driven out small merchants within a large geographical radius everywhere they've opened, and they're now open almost everywhere. Only the most loyal patron still shops at her local nursery when she can pay half as much for this season's daffodils a few extra miles away. And even if she stays loyal to the end, the end of that nursery comes quickly when there are not enough of her kind—and there never are.

In science, the "chaos" theory attempts to connect the flapping wings of a butterfly in Calcutta with rain, or the lack of it, in the Sonoran desert. I don't understand the physics, only the concept. But I do understand that the presence of a big-box store nine miles away from Main Street drove Lou's Hardware and Al's Tire Repair out of business, while the outflow of manufacturing jobs to offshore plants was responsible for the closing of Da Silva's Bricks and Johnson's Diner—where Da Silva's employees ate lunch. Every time I go back to my hometown of Bridgeport, Connecticut, which used to be one of America's great manufacturing hubs, I see the sad results of all the plant closings on the spokes of that hub. Our economy is like an intricate pattern of dominoes, except that people's lives and jobs and standard of living are the pieces. And as those dominoes fall, so do others that would seem, on the surface, not to be directly related.

Like education.

From what I can see, part of the collateral damage in the loss of communities has been the decline in our educational system. Over the last twenty years, but particularly in the last ten, control of the curriculum has shifted toward Washington in almost exactly the same way that local retailing has been replaced by mass merchants (and local manufacturing has required a requiem mass). Our public schools and public educators aren't making the grade—and that's not just measured by what our kids don't know about reading and math.

Which is why I'm so concerned. I'm concerned about the

failure of the public schools and teachers to prepare our children for productive lives. These days, the emphasis in public schools is on standardized testing, with students spending most of their time learning, or attempting to learn, exactly what these standardized tests say they should know before moving on to the next grade or graduating. Thinking and reasoning—which I'd always believed were the real skills that school was supposed to teach—are apparently no longer goals of the curriculum. Improved test scores may make a good headline every year and give people a chance to rejoice, but it's a shortsighted and ultimately futile gesture if our children can't think for themselves.

I heard a story recently about a man whose company sent him to assess an office in the Philippines, to see whether they should do business with that company. The first thing he noticed when he got there was a middle-aged woman, well-dressed, with her hands inside the back of a desktop computer. The man asked his Philippine host what she was doing. "Oh," he said, "she's one of our telephone salespeople. It looks like her computer is broken."

To which the American executive said, "Why doesn't she wait for the IT guy to fix it?"

"We don't have an IT department," the Filipino said. "Everybody has to be able to do everything."

On his first day back in the office in the United States, the American saw a young man staring—literally—at a blank computer screen. The executive inquired.

"This computer doesn't work," said the man.

"Did you call IT?"

"Uh, well, I put a note in the suggestion box."

There you have it—as good an example of a useless brain, one that hasn't ever learned to think, as you'll hear. My theory of why that brain exists, besides our inferior public education system, is that the further we get from an agrarian or seafaring society, the less capable people become. In agrarian societies, there was a direct correlation between your literal survival and what you knew, what you could do, and how creatively or ingeniously you solved problems. We've come so far from those days, I wouldn't be surprised to hear that millions of people believe corn grows in a can. For the love of vindaloo, we've had to outsource our problem-solving capabilities to customer helplines in India.

And yet our schools are cutting down or completely eliminating shop classes that could teach useful skills to students, especially those who aren't college material anyway—skills that they could use to make a good living. In my book, the manual arts always has and always will take precedence over the fine arts. Everything physical that the fine arts depend on—from theaters to canvases to printing and binding—depends on the manual arts. Educators who make the rules have bought into the popular notion that we've moved out of an industrial economy and into an information age, and therefore, they think, every student has to be educated in the same cookie-cutter way that ignores the importance of manual skills. They believe that in the future, everyone will wear a white collar—metaphorically speaking, of course. So as they fund high school curricula, they leave little or no money for shop. Yet in my travels to factories and in talks with factory owners, I hear one complaint more than any other: "We don't have enough skilled workers to fill our jobs."

And we're talking about good jobs—jobs that used to be filled by students who had more aptitude for the manual than the intellectual. There was no shame in it. In fact, being a great craftsman in my high school got you at least as many back pats as being a great intellect. And getting that great paycheck after high school for what you built with your hands got you a lot more than back pats. It bought you a wonderful life.

The truth is that our nation was built on our factories and the products they turn out. It was built on our communities that formed around those factories. It was built around the people who worked in the factories and their families. It was built on a foundation of common values and goals. Which is why I'm concerned, frankly, that this whole model of representative democracy and individual liberty called the United States will end with either a bang or a whimper. My guess is that it'll topple, because that's what eventually happens to structures whose foundations are relentlessly chipped away.

Saving it, one piece at a time, begins with hard work. And reversing the trend begins with each of us recognizing that we have the power, individually and collectively, to change where we're headed. The first step comes with an appreciation for our role in the fabric of America, and an awareness of where our money will end up every time we buy something. Great prices are wonderful—unless they cost too much. Just think about it. Every time you buy.

WHEN NO ONE IS LOOKING

★ ★ ★

There are some streets in America not made for the colossal RVs of the kind in which my TV crew and I travel. And there are some RV drivers who prefer their instincts to both a map and the advice of a hometown boy.

The mystery of what happens when these phenomena collide was solved for me early in my show's second season, on our way to visiting Derecktor Shipyards in Bridgeport, Connecticut—my hometown. The shotgun seat of the RV was a good place from which to watch the action. And reaction.

I advised "Eddie"—a name devised to protect the guilty—that he should turn left here before going right there, but Eddie insisted on turning right here before going straight there. After all, he was from Helena, Montana, and had never been to Bridgeport, which is the kind of logic that would make sense if you worked in Hollywood.

The dead end wasn't exactly a brick wall or misplaced factory; it was a gradual narrowing of the street that even the O. J. jurors could see would soon lead to an immovable object. In this case, the irresistible force that challenged it was Eddie's will. Thinking that we were witness to an optical illusion, he didn't stop when he might've still been able to back up easily into the intersection. No, the man barreled ahead as if we were on a Montana interstate until we'd reached the seam. Good thing the RV hadn't gotten that new coat of paint or we'd have been wedged between a 1951 Pontiac and a 1952 elm.

"Huh," Eddie snorted. "Hmmm. Ooh."

He stared at the ugly reality like he wanted to change the channel. *Where's that damn remote?*

"We must've gone the wrong way," he finally concluded.

We?

Eddie was apparently incapable of figuring a way out of this, and I'm glad of it, because it turned out to be one of those things that makes you believe in divine intelligence, if you're inclined that way. And I am.

He backed up just enough—slowly—to let me squeeze out the door so that I could be his eyes on the street. I walked behind, calling out directions as the RV reversed, and the further I got the more familiar this street became. I'd been on it before, I soon realized, several times when I was about nine—which would've been in about 1955.

Winter. Some kid—I don't remember his name or whether I even knew it then—threw a snowball at me on the way home from school. I threw one at him. Then the chase was on, laughing and running, the hunter becoming the hunted. Fun stuff. Then came my last snowball—a five-megaton weapon of war—launched the moment he reached his back door.

A glass door.

Would the snowball get there before it closed? *Please door, don't close yet. Please.*

Wham! There was a crash as the snowball put a clean hole the size of my fist in the thin glass . . . and then a louder crash as the glass around it gave way.

Now what? *Do I stay and face the music, or do I run away as fast as I can and never look back, because, come on, I don't know this kid, he doesn't know me, so I can get away with it?*

Tough choice. All right, not so tough. I ran. Fast. Laughing. Laughing harder the closer I got to home, realizing no one was behind me. *They'll never find me now.*

As soon as I walked in the door I could hear my mom on the telephone: "He did what?!"

That's right. That's the way the country worked back then, not just in Bridgeport but everywhere. The kid's mom didn't know me, but another mom who'd seen the whole thing did, and she knew that first mom. All those moms, a network of them—organic neighborhood watch teams, every mom's eyes on the street, aware of everything. In summer, fall, and spring, they'd be on the porch or visiting with each other. In winter, their curtains were open, their eyes scanning the public places. The only technology was the telephone, but they could call each other and pin down culprits faster than any Google search. No street was safe for scofflaws, because you could reasonably assume that every mother, every family, had the same values your family did.

So what changed that?

Television.

Suddenly, our backs were to the windows, attention on that box in the middle of the room instead of on anything happening outside. "Whose car is that?" was replaced by "What time is my show on?"—which used to be the question asked only at night, when the family was at home. But by the time I was in junior high school, well, you could get away with almost anything on the street in the daytime. Either the mothers who used to keep an eye on the street and each other were now watching *Edge of Night*, or they'd entered the workforce. I don't know if there's a connection between them; I only know that it's suspiciously coincidental.

So what was my punishment for breaking the window? It wasn't punishment, per se. It was an early lesson in responsibility with a little misery mixed in to make the lesson stick. Not having enough money to pay for the fix, I asked Dad to float me a loan. He said he wouldn't, which meant I had to solve the problem some other way. I ended up making a deal with the kid's father to work off the window by shoveling their sidewalk and walkway until I'd earned the amount it cost him. Apparently, though, my wage was about a dime an hour—which is where the misery part came in—because it took me most of the winter. I'd get up at five o'clock on snowy mornings, of which there were a lot, this being a particularly harsh winter, and trudge over there before school. Sometimes I was still shoveling when the kid I'd thrown the snowball at left for class. He only smirked at me the first time. Suffice it to say, he was a fast learner. But back then, we all were.

Eddie finally got the RV back to the intersection. Fresh from reliving the experience, I jumped inside and told him the broken-window story. "Geez, that's too bad," he said. "My dad would've given me the money."

"I know," I said.

TV OR NOT TV

★　★　★

Every year the Museum of Television and Radio in Los Angeles offers a series of seminars about certain television shows, giving fans an opportunity to watch an episode on a giant screen in an auditorium and then ask its stars, producers, and writers any questions they might have. It's a popular annual rite, and the presentations sell out quickly—or at least they did some years ago when a friend who was doing research for a project asked me to accompany him to the seminar for *Star Trek: The Next Generation*, a show I'd actually never seen.

It's true that some *Star Trek* fans have a reputation for eccentricity—for example, wearing Captain Kirk uniforms and Spock ears while speaking Klingon in court. But judging by their suitable clothing and their ability to articulate questions—as well as their capacity for coming up with twenty-five bucks a ticket—the audience on this night was composed of sophisticated and intelligent people. Granted this rare opportunity to pose questions to four of the show's actors and five of its writer-producers, they inquired thoughtfully into the characters' motivations, recent and future story lines, dialogue, alien customs, and other plans.

The problem was, they directed these questions to the actors, not to the writers or producers. How could series lead Patrick Stewart, for example, explain why he hadn't blasted someone with his phaser gun in a particular episode?

Each time the question was referred by the actor to one of the writers, and then would come the next question—again directed to an actor: "Will you be visiting the planet Ziptor again in a coming episode?"

There were, in fact, no questions that the actors were capable of answering properly—like, "Do you worry about being typecast in science fiction stories?" The repeated referrals to the brain trust became a running gag that got funnier each time, at least to the nine men and women on stage. From what I could tell in the audience, few seemed to get the joke.

In fact, on the way out that night, someone stopped me. "Hey, Cliff," he said. "Where's Norm?"

Par for the course.

Well, look, my mother didn't raise any dummies, so I'm aware that the reason you're reading this book—and the reason a major publisher asked me to write it—is that I'm recognizable and more or less famous, having come into your living room for about twenty-five years now. It goes without saying that I'm grateful to television for the opportunities it's given me and the life it's afforded me.

And yet I have my reservations about television in the same way that I have reservations about toast. I love toast. Matter of fact, I eat it every morning—with peanut butter. But I do try to eat to live rather than live to eat. Which means I hold myself to a single piece and leave off the top layer of cheddar.

That the toast comes out of a machine—the toaster—is analogous to programs coming out of the television set. Too much toast isn't good, and too many programs are bad. Too much is too much under any circumstances.

"Oh, but you make your living in TV," people say to me.

"Right," I say, "and if I made my living as a baker, would you expect me to eat cookies all day?"

When my children were little, I spliced a toggle switch in the cable line that no one but me knew about. Every time I thought they'd been devoting more time and attention than seemed healthy to that hypnotic tube, I'd slip outside and flip the switch, thus rendering the screen full of snow.

"Dad!" they'd scream. "The cable's out again."

"Yeah, go figure," I'd sympathize. "I'll call the cable guy."

"Boy," they'd moan, "none of our friends' houses have this problem. Our cable's always broken."

"Well, in the meantime, why don't you guys go outside and play."

Then a day or two later one of the kids would ask if I'd called the cable guy. "Oh, sure," I'd say, "he's coming Thursday."

Then Thursday would come: "He's missing a part. Has to be sent from Chicago or somewhere."

After two or three days of no TV, the board games would come out, and they'd be getting along better. And by then, they'd stop asking for the TV (which would come back on when *I* wanted to see something—and soon would begin the new cycle). You see, I didn't have to be the bad guy. And they were better off—their minds eating the equivalent of only a single piece of toast rather than the whole loaf. (Today, one's a college student and one's a high school senior, and both would rather do than watch, so I guess the strategy worked—though I can't wait to see how they react when they read my admission for the first time.)

Back in the tumultuous sixties, when television was still something of a novelty and public intellectuals could become pop icons, a Canadian professor named Marshall McLuhan coined a phrase about television that's as quotably memorable as anything uttered during the whole decade, even if the line was frequently misunderstood: "The medium is the message." At the time, most people believed that television was the messenger, not the message. But time has proved McLuhan to be a prophet.

Television dominates American life in a way nothing else ever has. Through an unending parade of images that create a kind of mesmerizing effect, it disassembles and reconstructs reality for millions of people who often believe that television itself *is* reality. Anything on the tube seems authentic, and anything not on seems unreal.

In other words: TV, therefore I am.

Just consider that there are more televisions than there are telephones in American homes, and that the vast majority of homes have more than one television; many, in fact, have a TV in every room, including the bathroom.

Of course, televisions are also in our classrooms, supermarkets, ball parks, airports, and plazas. They're in our cell phones and iPods and computers. Indeed, there's nowhere you can go—at least nowhere where there are other people—to escape television. TV shows us what to eat, wear, buy, and think; how to speak; and whom to admire and revile. It is the Supreme Court of values, celebrity, and news.

But it wasn't always so. Nor was it intended to be.

From the birth of commercial television in the late 1940s through the 1950s, the number of television sets in American living rooms rose exponentially. Wrapped in wonderful big boxes that promised big wonderful surprises, television made radio look old and puny. Almost as soon as television showed up, the contest ended. Radio may have been theater for the mind, but television was a feast for the eye. Since the average person preferred watching ten pictures to hearing ten thousand words, radio's audience shrank as television sales boomed. And radio's proudest cultural draws, like NBC's Arturo Toscanini–led symphony and the popular dramas that for three decades had gathered the family around the Philco, disappeared almost overnight. Many of them were reborn on television. The difference, though, was that television was innately passive entertainment, whereas radio had been active, requiring imagination and concentration. No matter how many hours of radio you listened to, you couldn't possibly be called a "couch potato."

At first because of its novelty, and then later because it asked for nothing from its viewers other than their eyeballs, television was like a torrent of nature, gobbling up everything in its path, reshaping the American landscape in ways that even the four years of World War II had not.

Restaurants and nightclubs went out of business. Sporting venues suffered with lower attendance figures. Cab drivers earned less money per nighttime shift. Public libraries reported decreases in circulation, and book sales dropped by a similar rate. People were just staying home to stare at the box—before, during, and after dinner (which might now be a Swanson's frozen TV meal, heated and served on a TV tray in the living room ten feet from the tube). It wasn't the programming as much as television itself: the mere idea of electronically magnetized particles coming together into entertaining images seemed nothing less than miraculous. And free.

Movie theaters fared worst of all. "Closed Tuesday," said the sign in the Ohio theater window, 1950. "I want to see Berle, too." But even against less popular shows than Uncle Miltie's, movies couldn't compete. In 1951, when the national drop in movie attendance averaged more than 30 percent, 131 theaters closed in Southern California, 64 in Chicago, and 55 in metro New York. The more television stations in a city—that is, the more viewing choices—the fewer the number of movie tickets sold.

Theater owners had originally dismissed television as a passing fancy, but they soon realized that their competition was never going to go away. No wonder. TV didn't ask anything of its viewers. People who used to get dressed and go out to see movies twice a week were now watching on their own couches every night, seduced by moving pictures that came into their living rooms at the flip of a switch.

Television was America's Svengali. We fell under its spell, imitated what we saw, and bought what we saw advertised. In just two years, 1950 to 1952, sales of Hazel Bishop lipstick went from $50,000 annually to $4.5 million—because the company paid for its message to be seen on television.

In fact, being on television conferred a kind of legitimacy unprecedented in history. The words "As seen on TV" soon began showing up in print advertising as the ultimate seal of approval, and the words got results, because most people believed that what they saw was somehow filtered for truth and value.

But the words work today too, though we know better, because television has become its own truth. There's no other way to explain the family I read about some years ago who refused to be rescued from rising floodwaters around their home because they couldn't take their five televisions with them in the firefighters' rowboat. "They're all we've got," the man of the house said, "and we don't have insurance. So if we can't save 'em, we're not going."

Truly, television's domination or influence, or whatever word you prefer, has little to do with the actual programs flickering from our screens. We watch because it's there, and whatever we watch assumes outsized importance. Which means that, even for the minority who don't watch much, reality is still reshaped by the hundreds of millions who do. All of popular culture—from music to magazines, radio to ballet, movies to opera—reflects television's blue light. As do politics, education, and relationships. If you want to sell more magazines, put a TV celebrity on the cover. If you're a legislator wanting to draw press to your pet cause or subcommittee, get a TV celebrity to testify as an expert.

Everyone who saw the commercial that began "I'm not a doctor, but I play one on TV" got the joke. But the ad genius who wrote that line to sell aspirin wasn't joking. He knew that a TV actor identifying himself as such probably carried more cachet than a real doctor because he could better hold our short attention span.

Rather than integrating television into our lives, we've integrated our lives into television's 24-hour day, using TiVo and On Demand to mainline the programming into our brains.

Today's reality is about a million miles from the hopes of TV's pioneers. This new technology, capable of reaching into the average home with both sound and pictures, was intended to serve our noblest aims and goals. More than radio and the movies, television had the power to bring the world to the common man and connect us all to a common experience. It was going to educate, enrich, and ennoble us—at least in their imaginations.

That's why, in the 1950s, the Federal Communications Commission sponsored public dialogues to help determine what role the new medium should play in a free society. One frequent topic was commercialization—whether a sponsor's influence might undermine television's potential for doing good. How quaint to think now that that sort of thing was actually debated in earnest.

And how quaint that, once upon that same time, stations were compelled by law to devote a certain number of hours to programming in the "public interest." While the term may have been hard to define exactly, we knew it when we saw it, and the concept was considered practical. That these pictures came into our living rooms over public airwaves ("belonging to everyone") implied both responsibility and obligation. Broadcasters, it was felt, were merely leasing some bandwidth, which was why stations that wanted their licenses renewed—that is, *every* station—had to demonstrate to the FCC's satisfaction that they had served the public interest and not violated the public trust.

There were religious programs on Sunday mornings, Saturday-afternoon announcements of local relevance, and a sign-off prayer followed by the national anthem. On-air announcements encouraged critical letters from viewers, presumably to be included in the relicensing proposal. And whether or not renewal was in fact all but automatic, the licensees tried to avoid offense as much as possible and did indeed serve the public interest according to the mores of the era. It was in that context that some people asserted television would be the vessel to lift us above what was then referred to as a "rising tide of mediocrity."

Newton Minow, the FCC's chairman in the late fifties and early sixties, had once been one of those people. But seeing that television was in part responsible for this rising tide, he famously called it a "vast wasteland." Almost fifty years later, the term seems like a ridiculous exaggeration, if only because the perfection of his description left us no comparable catchphrase to adequately describe the cesspool that much of television has become since then.

An important point, made no less important by being obvious, is that the creative people who originally shaped television didn't have television as a cultural heritage. That's not to say that they'd been exposed only to high-brow entertainment necessarily. But in their era, which encompassed the Depression and World War II, when a primary leisure activity was reading and conversation was considered an art, the cultural touchstones were the golden ages of both Broadway and Hollywood. That's why a stage revival was likely to be *Hamlet*, and no studio would consider naming a movie, say, *Dumb and Dumber.* If you doubt the point, consider that in 1955 a biography of George Bernard Shaw sold a sensational 250,000 copies—even though book sales had already started to decline, thanks to TV's growing lure.

That was the kind of yardstick Newton Minow measured television against when he proclaimed it a wasteland. Apparently he was too idealistic, having an imagination inadequate to conceive of how high the mediocrity was yet to rise—high enough to make it unthinkable that an equivalent book would sell a tenth of that number today, even with 75 million more potential buyers. ("George Bernard Who?" would likely be the question.)

When the typical American spends nearly as much time watching TV every day as he does sleeping—and attention spans are presumed to last as long as a single music-video image—what can you reasonably expect? Well, you can expect feature films made from nearly every old television series, political candidates measured by their screen personas and performances instead of their ideas, and print advertising that proudly declares "As seen on TV."

I can't believe that any of television's first-generation architects—not CBS chairman William S. Paley, nor NBC chairman David Sarnoff—ever anticipated the medium taking on such a vivid life of its own, apart from the world it was supposed to serve. Now television magnifies trivia and trivializes reality. Having become our master, television gives the thumbs-up or thumbs-down to our experiences the way Roman emperors did to gladiators and Christians.

To millions, television images are now more legitimate than the light of day. Without TV's validation, they mistrust what they see—like the woman I encountered while walking through the opening of the Tattoo Museum in Laguna Beach sometime back. She had a video camera seemingly glued to her eye, so I and everyone else there assumed she was another of the many news reporters. Only later, when she kept the camera affixed to her eye even while chit-chatting with others over beer and brownies, were we disabused of that notion. I asked her what she was recording. Aiming the camera at me, she said, "Nothing. Things just look better to me this way."

Such absurdities occur frequently enough to be considered a trend. A few years ago a Southern California mental health agency run by a friend of a friend held a fund-raising dinner at which the two guests of honor were Marlo Thomas and Marie Balter. Thomas had recently won an Emmy for portraying Balter, a woman who'd spent nearly thirty years in a mental institution because of a misunderstanding and a misdiagnosis.

Released from the institution in her fifties, Balter went on to earn a master's degree from Harvard and become a professional mental-health advocate. Great story, right? Inspiring, yes? Well, throughout the evening's festivities, Marlo Thomas was surrounded by attendees congratulating her portrayal, which she graciously attributed entirely to Balter—who, alas, sat most of evening alone at her table, ignored by these same people.

Today's answer to the question of whether a tree makes noise when it falls in the forest: only when cameras are there.

★ Thirteen years ago, when she was about to turn forty, my friend Lisa got suddenly depressed. She thought her best years were behind her and felt anguished about her recent divorce.

To cheer her up, Lisa's best friend Elaine decided to throw a black-tie surprise party. She invited Lisa's twenty favorite friends and told them to show up no later than six—half an hour before Lisa was coming to pick up Elaine for "a quiet dinner alone, so we can talk."

The party fell on a warm night. Elaine awaited her guests on the front walkway, which she'd covered in red carpeting. Trying to make the affair seem like the arrival of the stars for the Academy Awards, she wore a rented Armani tux and held a microphone connected to a video camera operated by her husband, Tom. When each person stepped onto the carpet, Elaine stuck out the microphone and conducted a brief interview about Lisa, and like the real pre-Oscars rite, most of the answers were uninspired—though they were dutifully recorded anyway for Lisa's amusement later. After the last of us had completed the routine, everyone went inside to await her arrival.

It was a big moment: shock, embarrassment, laughter, tears,

back to laughter. Tom caught Lisa's full reaction on video, as well as the following twenty cinema verité minutes of us milling around, pouring drinks, eating snacks, waving to the camera.

As soon as Tom put down the camera, Elaine stuck the cassette into her VCR and called Lisa in to watch. Everyone else followed and immediately gathered around the television, staking out positions on the couches and floor. Though the party had barely begun, everyone was already watching themselves on TV—apparently to see if they'd been having a good time so far.

I admit I thought this was absurd. It would've been one thing to wait till the end of the night to watch—say, after the food and cake. But to have the party be about watching ourselves rather than actually interacting—that is, having a real party—seemed beyond beyond.

As these things sometimes happen when the gods are smiling, I noticed a Polaroid camera in a bookcase. Luckily, it was loaded with a full cartridge, so over the next half hour I snapped half a dozen photos of faces staring at the TV. No one even appeared bothered by the flash. They were too absorbed.

When the video ended and everyone began milling around again, I began handing out the photos one by one. They were passed around the room, igniting small explosions of laughter. By the time all six photos filled the pipeline, people were grabbing each for a third and fourth viewing, and the convulsion drowned out the rock music in the background.

Sensing one of those golden opportunities, I again picked up the Polaroid and snapped more shots, this time of them studying the photos of them watching the video of themselves. They could hardly wait for each new shot to develop completely before snatching it. Everyone hurt from laughing, and I used the remaining film on more photos.

Soon the Polaroid was empty, but the joke wasn't over. At some point Tom had picked up his video camera and recorded the scene of them laughing at photos of them laughing at photos of them laughing at photos . . . of them laughing at themselves on video.

It quickly became obvious that the only thing people really wanted to do now was watch the new footage. And so we did. And that was basically the party. Happy fortieth, Lisa.

In a way, though, it was the perfect fortieth birthday party, given that Lisa—like everyone else at the party, myself included—was a Baby Boomer who'd watched herself grow up on television and whose worldview was shaped in whole or part by TV.

Actually, the real story of my generation's relationship to TV began around the time that Philo T. Farnsworth, age fourteen, was tilling a potato field and had the sudden insight that electron beams could scan images one line at a time, just like your eyes reading a book. And thus was born, at least in concept, the television picture tube. The year was 1920, when millions of kids, better known as Baby Boomers' parents, were being born. (Farnsworth's first working model would take another seven years.) After surviving the Depression and World War II, two events that were not for the faint of heart, they vowed that their own children, better known as us, would not suffer as they had. And indeed, thanks to their epidemic of prosperity, we Boomers wanted for little—at least compared to every previous generation since Ramses III led off the 20th Dynasty. By the time we'd grown to become the largest generation, we were already the most indulged.

It wasn't just our parents indulging us, either. All of popular culture was learning to remake itself in the image of, and pander to, kids with money. (We first joined the word "popular" to culture.) Radio had a renaissance by playing music sung by and about teenage angst. Movies, too, tried to save themselves from oblivion by aiming at young people (all the "B" science fiction with high school protagonists). And while teen films didn't dominate late-1950s movie screens the way teen music dominated the AM dial, it's no coincidence that three of the decade's films referred to most often as "seminal" are *The Wild One*, *Rebel Without a Cause*, and *Blackboard Jungle*—which, of course, are all about teenage rebellion (but that's another topic).

Television hit the jackpot. In 1955, *The Mickey Mouse Club*'s Annette and Darlene and Cubby looked just like most of the millions of (white) kids watching them, as did the kids screaming for Elvis on Ed Sullivan's stage a year later, and the kids dancing on *American Bandstand* a year after that. So, too, did Wally and Beaver, the Nelson boys, and Bud, Kitten, and Princess.

Seeing themselves on it, young (white) people perceived television as a mirror of America. If they'd had an adult's perspective, they might not have inferred the message that television was built to capture their coming of age, like some sort of home movie to which radio was the soundtrack. But they did.

And they had good reason to.

Everywhere on television, the same old snake oil was being pitched by a younger salesman. "Mothers are like that. Yeah, they are," the boy on that now-famous Bayer aspirin commercial declared. Whenever possible, sponsors put young people into their advertising, while ads for products aimed at older people began focusing on looking and acting "young again." This worship of youth was unique in history. The networks even began talking about demographics to advertisers.

No matter that a lot of television programming ignored

young people. The point is that attention followed wherever young people paid attention. What they watched created a spotlight—and with light came heat. When teen fans of *77 Sunset Strip* embraced "Kookie," actor Edd Byrnes became "hot," and the novelty ode to him, "Kookie (Lend Me Your Comb)," was one of 1960's "hot" sellers.

If nothing else, television had become a star-maker. Successful careers didn't always begin on television, but they usually ended without it. Entertainers of every ilk—from movie stars to crooners, poets to dancers—now knelt at television's throne and kissed the ring. By then, of course, young people believed that the ring adorned their own finger, which they promptly raised to the world.

Today's young people think of television as either a window into their own province or a magic mirror that tells them what they want to hear. Either way, television produces the type of confusion I saw (on TV) and will never forget. A woman was trying to get a seat inside a South Carolina courthouse where the jury was being chosen for the trial of Susan Smith, the mother who, a decade ago, blamed a carjacker for kidnapping her two young sons but then later admitted to drowning them.

"I don't know what this all means," the woman told a TV reporter, "but it sure beats the soap operas at home."

★ In 1961, nothing typified the "era of optimism," as the newspapers called it, like new President John Kennedy's announcement that America would land a man on the moon (and bring him home again) by the end of the decade. It was a declaration of infinite horizons and new rules.

Kennedy initiated the space race because he realized that

the prestige of the United States rested on outdoing our geo-political and philosophical rival, the Soviet Union. He remembered how foolish Eisenhower had looked after Moscow beat us to orbit with Sputnik. He remembered the 1960 Olympics in Rome and the '56 Games in Melbourne, when, for the first time, the Soviets had won more gold medals than the United States.

Under Kennedy's watch there would be none of that. As he battled the ghost of Truman's losing China to the Communists, he insisted that the United States emerge with a clear victory on a field of endeavor that would allow us to prove our mettle: science. While war provided a more direct comparison, only sci-ence, under the guise of a dramatic race, could demonstrate so graphically the fruits of freedom and free enterprise. Just as they'd produced better supermarkets and washing machines, they'd surely produce better rocketry.

Kennedy was shrewd enough to credit his slim victory over Nixon to telegenic charm. He clearly grasped the power of tele-vision and understood that if his space drama was to capture America's hearts and minds, it would require live heroes—he-roes we could get to know, up close and personal, on television. In private meetings with the heads of the three networks, Kennedy lobbied for real-time coverage of the launches. Re-luctantly at first, they eventually agreed.

Our guys conquering space became America's first collec-tively shared moments since FDR's fireside chats—but those had been "just" radio. For each launch and landing, we riveted ourselves in front of screens, either at home or outside store windows with dozens of others. Televisions were even brought into classrooms, and, as Kennedy had foreseen, astronauts like John Glenn and Scott Carpenter became household names— and faces. Over the following decade, the "race to the moon" began to seem like a long-running series, one that later culminated in the worldwide broadcast of Neil Armstrong stepping onto the lunar surface.

One by-product of NASA's bottomless checkbook was AT&T's Telstar communications satellite. To Kennedy, the satellite's importance as a symbol of American superiority overshadowed even its capability: to watch in Duluth what was happening right now in Istanbul (or to watch in Peoria was what happening on the moon). He pushed through approval of a NASA launch, ignoring the ethical questions raised about having both tax dollars and a government agency benefiting AT&T. Meanwhile he championed and then signed into law the Communications Satellite Act to encourage global participation through ground stations in many countries.

Telstar's first broadcast in 1962 was an historic moment—more historic, more important, than the driving of the golden spike at Promontory or the first transcontinental phone call. After all, if Telstar had been there, those events would have been *seen*.

Hey, this was television. Everything before its existence seemed merely quaint, if not medieval. (No wonder kids pitied their parents and grandparents, who hadn't grown up with television back in the "olden days.")

Commentator David Brinkley mocked that attitude during the first broadcast when he stood in NBC's Paris studio and declared, "Live, via Telstar, there is no important news to report."

As Brinkley later discovered, fewer people than he had hoped understood his witty remark. Television itself was the story now and would remain so; to viewers, nothing on the screen meant everything. "What can it do?" That was the question being asked, not whether what it could do was a good thing to be done. We were in the age of progress. And progress, as General Electric's television commercials insisted, was "our most important product."

Progress came to the networks in the form of expanded evening newscasts, from fifteen minutes to a half hour. Filling those extra minutes were pictures from here and afar whose newsworthiness was secondary to availability. Broadcasting them because they could be seen was considered progress.

Now that television aimed to show more than tell, television news had to distinguish itself from radio and newspapers—and talking heads staring into the camera to report the events of the day weren't distinguished enough. So instead of correspondents discussing famine in the Ukraine, we watched ballooning accidents in the Alps. Instead of Mao's purges, we saw footage of urban crime scenes.

Soon, no story without a video eyewitness could lead the newscast, and in short order, few stories lacking footage were reported at all. Where the camera couldn't go, the networks didn't follow. And since people weaned on television had concluded that the camera is always present wherever an important story breaks, they believed that anything not covered was unimportant. So, just thirty years after the Holocaust, America all but ignored the killing fields of Cambodia (which didn't quite have First Amendment freedom of the press). And twenty years later we were able to ignore the genocide in Rwanda, followed in ten years by the slaughter in Darfur—all because television cameras weren't allowed access.

Israel, however, has few restrictions on reporters, so I'm able to vividly recall an incident in the early 1990s when an Israeli soldier shot and killed a Palestinian who was raising a ruckus over Israel's presence on the West Bank. The story, complete with footage of demonstrations on both sides, occupied the first several minutes of the network news program I was watching and was the banner headline the next morning on the front page of both the *Los Angeles Times* and the *New York Times*.

Okay, fine. News is news, right? But on the same day, another story, this one from Brazil, merited only a three-inch dispatch from the Reuters news agency in the *New York Times*—and was utterly ignored everywhere else, including and especially by the network news programs. What was the story? Three hundred Brazilian Indians who'd been demonstrating against government encroachment on their tribal lands were herded by army troops onto and then over a bridge, falling to their deaths. In other words, a mass murder of political intent.

Now, isn't that a more newsworthy story than one death in a war that had been going on for fifty years? You'd think so, but you'd be wrong.

The difference between these stories is that television cameras had recorded one of them and not the other. Ergo, the other is undeserving of our attention.

No doubt the reason riots consumed Los Angeles for the better part of a week in the spring of 1992 was that an amateur video cameraman happened to record Rodney King's beating. That enabled the news stations to show the footage over and over, even though the context for which the beating had taken place couldn't possibly have been determined by the video. It inflamed passions, as television does—which is why, ironically, we almost never see footage of the planes hitting the World Trade Center towers or of the falling bodies of those who had to choose on that September morning between death by incineration and death by jumping a hundred stories. News directors, in their infinite wisdom, have decided that the populace would become too inflamed by repetition of the images in their vaults. Too bad they didn't decide similarly about Rodney King.

I remember almost inhaling my mustache a couple of times during the L.A. riots, when looters would pause to grant interviews to television reporters (just as they did in New Orleans, after Hurricane Katrina). Their arms laden with stolen merchandise, they unashamedly admitted that after taking all they could carry, they'd go home to unload their booty and watch live coverage in order to pinpoint the next hot looting spot. Smiling, some of them even asked whether their interviews would be replayed later, on tape delay, so that they could watch themselves.

It's entirely plausible that Vietnam was lost after the war began appearing nightly in our living rooms. By 1968's Tet offensive, when the antiwar protests reached critical mass, America's young people had been watching television all their lives. Which made Vietnam seem like just another long-running series, one that "starred" bombs, napalm, dead bodies, and somber reporters. So they couldn't understand the fighting in the context of either the geopolitical cold war or the lessons of Korea; instead, they judged Vietnam against *Leave It to Beaver* and *Dr. Kildare*—shows in which resolution followed conflict in thirty or sixty minutes. That's what they were used to, and it's what they weren't getting from Vietnam. No wonder they petitioned to have the series canceled. And so it was.

Television's coverage of Vietnam raises the question of whether World War II would have turned out differently if Morley Safer and Peter Arnett had been there to feed daily pictures back home for dinnertime consumption. Actually, it raises the issue of whether *any* war can be prosecuted fully when its horrors are witnessed by a constituency holding a beer in one hand and remote control in the other.

That's what we have to answer now, as the Iraq war continues, brought to our televisions by reporters who were weaned on Vietnam and tend to see everything through that corrupt lens. They believe that the only story is the number of combat deaths, and not the wider conflict nor the genuine progress that's being made in much of the country in terms of infrastructure and economy and freedom of the press. Rare, to say the least, is the news image from Iraq that doesn't include something or someone blowing up.

I can't help thinking that, all things being equal, the coverage of thousands of deaths a day in World War II—more in one hour, sometimes, than the accumulated total so far of our brave troops in Iraq—would have demoralized Americans glued to the news of that war. A million ground troops, air superiority, and moral righteousness are, I suspect, no match for the unblinking camera.

So God bless television and all the joys it's brought. But as we watch, let's keep it in judicious perspective—just the way we try to do with those third and fourth pieces of toast. It may taste good going down, but eventually there's a price to be paid.

A TRACTOR WITH A VIEW

★   ★   ★

H ey, John, have you ever driven a tractor before?" the John Deere executive asked as we were walking through his factory's visitor center, a replica of a 1950s Deere dealership where they hold monthly auctions for gorgeous reconditioned equipment—like the 1960s green beauty he must've seen me eyeing.

Had I ever driven a tractor before?

Well, there was a long answer and a short answer. I gave him the short answer. I'll give you the long answer, because in it lies a worthy tale.

It was the early summer of 1969. I was hitching from Bridgeport to Canada to go backpacking. State troopers noticed the hippie standing with his thumb out on the shoulder of the New York State Thruway and kicked me off at Kingston before I could catch a ride.

The black sky said that a major storm was coming. Half a mile down the road I knocked on the door of a house whose front yard had a "Storage Sheds for Sale" sign, hoping to take shelter in one of them for the night. No one answered, so I sat on the porch; at least I'd be out of the rain when it started.

Soon a VW van drove up—a good sign; anyone in a van was part of the club. But it turned out not to be the house's owner, which I cleverly ascertained when the driver asked how much the storage sheds cost. I told him who I was and he drove away, then came back ten minutes later and said, "I'm Tony the Mime. It was wrong of me not to offer you a place to stay. Get in."

That's how it was done in the Age of Aquarius.

Off we went to Tony the Mime's place in Bearsville, a couple miles west of Woodstock. Just like that I moved in—which was also how it was done back in the day—exchanging carpentry for room and board and, most important, mime lessons. It's not that I wanted to be a mime necessarily, but at the time miming seemed like a useful life skill. You never knew when you'd have to pretend to be locked in a box.

I didn't stop to consider for even a moment how long I'd stay there. Maybe forever. Maybe till tomorrow. Plans? Feh. Plans were just a petit bourgeois plot foisted on the ignorant and unsuspecting by the ruling class in order to rob this moment, right now, of its infinite beauty—which was how "they" got everyone to show up at work every day and make them rich by keeping the giant capitalist machine humming. (Or something like that. I may be forgetting my dogma and cant.)

In those days, this all seemed so magnetically alluring, impossible to resist, even if it all ran contrary to everything I'd been raised to believe. My heroes then were Sartre and Camus and Kerouac—especially Kerouac. And my aim: an existential life. Authentic. On the road. The Dharma Bum himself. Today was the only day that counted. Oh, and tonight. Tonight especially.

One night I was down at the bar in town. I'd been there the night before, too, when Jimi Hendrix had walked in. Actually, I'd been there every night—like I said, Kerouac—and seen a lot of rock stars having a lot of drinks. America's rock idols had apparently heard that other rock stars were hanging out in the area made famous by Dylan and the Band, and none of them wanted to be left out of the hang, so the place was lousy with legends that all the town civvies came there to pretend not to see. You weren't supposed to notice, for example, that Dylan had just stepped on your toe or Stephen Stills had puked on your shirt, but when Hendrix came in I couldn't resist putting a dime in the jukebox and playing "Foxy Lady"—which was like farting in an elevator. As soon as the doors opened, he ran out.

Anyway, the next night some guy stood on the bar and announced there was going to be a huge rock festival on Max Yasgur's farm, and workers were needed to turn it into a temporary amphitheater for the fifty thousand or so hippies they expected to show up—the most ever at a rock concert. The pay, he promised, would be good.

To me, it sounded like a nice gig for a week or two, but when the guy left someone else said that the townsfolk were none too happy about the permits being granted, because they hated the hippies they already had and, despite granting the permit for a fee, didn't want to attract any more of them. In fact, he said, the townies were planning to kidnap a bunch of them and gather everyone in the town square for a mass haircut—the equivalent of a nonlethal lynching.

The hippie next to me confided that he'd already been having nightmares of waking up bald and shaved. He'd sit up in bed sweating, imagining life without his hair.

"I'd never get laid again," he predicted. "No way I'm going anywhere near that place."

I commiserated. My hair was a foot long, my beard thick enough to hide a small child, and yes, scoring without a freak flag waving in the wind would be difficult. But I braved the enemy lines anyway and showed up at the Woodstock Music and Art Fair hiring office, getting in line behind a dozen or so guys who looked like they were auditioning for the live-action movie of the underground comic book *Zap Comix;* they were dead ringers for the Fabulous Furry Freak Brothers, Mr. Natural, and Flaky Foont. In front of them waited a guy wearing a loin cloth on his head, flies buzzing around it. So even though I looked like Jeremiah Johnson six months out, by the time my turn came the hiring boss said, "You seem like you're pretty together. Can you drive a tractor?"

Well, he hadn't asked if *I had ever* driven a tractor. He asked if I could, which meant, *Can you learn to drive a tractor?*

"Sure I can," I said—because that was another thing in the Age of Aquarius: you knew you could do anything.

All I had to do was learn.

I walked outside into the huge field, which had evidently been covered by alfalfa before all this began, to find a beautiful green John Deere tractor sitting idle. I climbed up into the seat and turned the key. It purred. My assignment: to ferry two-by-twelves from the lumber pile over to where they were erecting the stage, maybe two hundred yards away, up on a rise.

Let's see, this baby's got a clutch and gears—so far so good. Now you just pop this out, and—uh-oh.

The tractor lurched and tipped backward, so I was suddenly on the down end of a seesaw, with my head almost touching the ground. No worries, though. A hippie who called
himself Mr. Green Jeans gave me a few pointers, and I soon
began hauling loads to the stage area.

On one of the first trips, I passed by an area near the stage
where a curly-haired guy wearing a leather vest with no shirt
had just gotten off a BSA motorcycle to talk to someone I recognized from Tony the Mime's classes. It was Joey, a hippie mer-
chant who sold his own head gear and silver and turquoise
jewelry. I overheard him say he wanted to set up a booth at the
festival, but then I pulled out of earshot and by the time I got
back from delivering the load, Joey and motorcycle man were
screaming at each other.

An hour later, when I met the curly-haired guy, Michael
Lang—one of the four Woodstock venture partners and therefore my boss—I wanted to compliment him on the beauty of
his right hook, which had completely clocked Joey. But I decided against it for the same reason you didn't play Hendrix's
music on the jukebox when Jimi walked in. Fistfights over
money and deals were one of those dead elephants that always
appeared on the floor when hippies and capitalism came together.

What elephant?

As it turned out, Lang and his partners showed a grasp of
PR and marketing that I didn't think hippies were supposed to
have. It seemed so, uh, Machiavellian and uncosmic to call the
festival "Woodstock," when in fact the site was really in Bethel,
in order to capitalize on Dylan's famous residence in the town.
Then I heard how they'd been building up the event in the underground press for months. Ads on hip FM stations across the
country announced that a ticket also bought a campsite, and

periodic messages called it a "weekend in the country" and a "temporary commune." The partners knew middle- and upper-class kids wanted in on the whole commune-ist thing but didn't want to suffer too much for their authenticity. That's why they hired an authentic commune organizer named Wavy Gravy to be their public voice and face—to make it seem like sleep-away camp but with better sex and without sadistic counselors.

Wavy's real name was Hugh Romney. Ten years before he'd been a beatnik comedian. A few years later he'd hooked up with Ken Kesey's Merry Pranksters. Now he was a toothless hippie who ran an outfit in New Mexico called the Hog Farm. About a hundred of his Hog Farmers and fifteen Hopi Indians from the land next to theirs were there as "the hippie police." I wondered why only fifty thousand hippie kids would need so many cops at a "festival of love and peace," same as I wondered why we'd cleared such a huge amount of acreage—enough to hold eight or ten times that many people.

The answers started coming on Thursday morning, a day and a half before the music was supposed to start.

People.

Loads of them.

Traffic backed up the ten miles from Route 17 to 17B. And by four that afternoon, twenty-five thousand people were camped out.

Wavy Gravy deputized anyone whose looks he liked, making them "security guards" and giving them a secret password—"I forget," which essentially made everyone there a security guard, because those were the two words most likely to be said by somebody spaced out on almost anything going around in those days.

"I'm a security guard. Are you?"

"I forget."

"Oh, so you are."

"I am what?"

"I don't know, I forget."

"What?"

★ On Friday morning Bethel residents woke up to see hippies sleeping in their backyards. Now Route 17B was backed up nine miles past Monticello, so there was no way the tow truck drivers who'd been hired to haul in ticket booths could get there.

So all of this—and there'd never be a dime collected at the gate.

Normally, you might have wondered what that could've meant for yourself and everyone else actually working the fair. But there was nothing normal about the summer of 1969. Men had just landed on the moon, sex was free, and everything was always "cool"—even the gruesome murders of Sharon Tate and four friends, whose blood had been used to write "Pig" on the walls, a week before.

Friday afternoon my tractor and I had just dropped off something needed for the stage's finishing touches when someone near me said, "Holy—."

From my perch on the tractor I could see way back, past the couple hundred thousand people already there, at what looked like a riot. But it was no such thing. It was the fences coming down, so that people wouldn't be herded through a gate and possibly get stampeded and crushed. I thought how ironic it was that the only people making money on this thing, besides the musicians who inspired us to revolution, were the hippies in makeshift booths selling pipes and Che posters and Mao's

Little Red Book. I couldn't help wondering why Joey wasn't among them when I pulled away from the back side of the stage and heard, "Jesus! Jesus!"

Some guy, his eyes flashing like he'd taken too much acid (how much is just enough?), was running alongside the tractor, trying to touch me.

I said, "You've got me confused with someone else."

"Jesus, it's you," he insisted. "Jesus, Jesus."

"Buddy, I'm not Jesus. I swear."

I sped up, and so did he, keeping pace.

"Please, Jesus. Jesus, Jesus."

He lunged for me, coming close to the small front wheel on the right. I would've veered left if there hadn't been a group of people in the way. Too late now. The huge back tire had started to roll up his leg just before I stopped, accidentally trapping him in the mud like an elongated banana peel.

I jumped down off my seat, sized up the situation. Even letting out the clutch to reverse would've lurched the tractor forward enough to send him directly for a meeting with the real Jesus. Luckily, I found a way to roll backwards without using the tractor's own power.

"Jesus," he said as he lay there—which, as a matter of fact, is exactly what I would've yelled if a tractor had just run over my leg. But he didn't mean it in that way.

And when I touched his leg everything was fine. It was a miracle. Really.

"Jesus," he said, and for a minute I . . . never mind.

★ When the show finally began, Richie Havens led off instead of Tim Hardin, because Hardin was too stoned and Havens either wasn't or didn't look it, which was why Michael Lang begged him to get out there ASAP and mollify the itchy crowd who'd been waiting since forever it seemed for the music to start. Any longer, he said, and they might've started throwing things—or rushing the stage. So Richie came out and strummed a hole through his guitar.

Then Lang asked him to stretch the hour into two hours, and the second hour into three, because about the only vehicles moving in the entire place were tractors and Lang's motorcycle. The performers couldn't get there except in helicopters, which were late and not big enough. The only helicopters that could accommodate the Jefferson Airplane or the Grateful Dead or any real kickass rock groups belonged to the U.S. Army, which spent the next three days ferrying musicians—and food and supplies—in and out of this "festival" populated, ironically, by hundreds of thousands of people who hated the helos and the people who flew them and what they allegedly stood for. Country Joe McDonald of Country Joe & the Fish confirmed exactly that, after Richie Havens nearly dropped of exhaustion, when he ran out on stage and prefaced his "I-Feel-Like-I'm-Fixin'-to-Die-Rag" with his anti–Uncle Sam and Vietnam "fish cheer."

As one the crowd shouted their favorite F word, then did it again and again as he bid, like a hallelujah congregation testifying at a perverse religious revival.

Standing beside the stage, I shivered when they crowd rose to their feet. If Country Joe had told them how cool it was to pillage the homes of the rich people in the next town, I think they might've rushed to do just that. Half a million people seemed to be of one mind, and that mind said that nothing from the past, no rules, applied anymore; the Year One began now. For a moment I felt terrified, and it occurred to me that the country would never again be the same.

Michael Wadleigh, the filmmaker whose crew was getting this all down, must've felt the same. He didn't really have a plan for what to do with all the footage, except for knowing that he didn't need any love songs—only the antiwar and antiestablishment stuff. That's what this was about; that was its significance. The fact that he'd gotten the money from a big corporation like Warner Brothers, which was going to distribute the film a year later and charge admission to see it, apparently didn't count.

At midnight it started raining—five inches in four hours—washing away the last semblance of propriety. Thousands of people rushed to wherever there might be shelter, knocking over tents and some of the lean-tos made of wood and tarps. It was terrifying to see the law of the jungle merging with the hippie law that said private property was public property the minute someone else wanted it, too.

In the deluge, the ground varied from pond-size puddles to flowing torrents that stripped away the topsoil on hard red clay and rock. From that night on, except for ferrying giant kettles of soup, my main job was to help build shelters. I also took people who'd cut their bare feet on broken glass or ignored advice by ingesting the brown acid to first-aid stations.

Some of the people in my tractor ambulance were having bad trips, seeing spiders on their skin, after taking the bad acid or drinking Kool-Aid that they didn't know was electric. Others had actually been on good trips—too good; they'd gone blind after losing a staring contest with the sun. On one drop-off at the medical tent I saw Jimi Hendrix lying on a cot, eyes closed. I thought he'd died—OD'ed maybe—and didn't even consider it news. *Hmm, Jimi Hendrix—dead. Yeah, makes sense.*

Meanwhile, trucks with food couldn't get in, and when word spread to the outside that the kids didn't have enough to eat, adults from around the area gathered in the Monticello Jewish Community Center with food from their pantries to make thousands of sandwiches that were then airlifted in. Other shipments followed, dozens of them, from all over, which arrived in National Guard helicopters. Too bad the kids who surrounded a food truck that was stuck a few miles away didn't have the same generous attitude. They held up the driver and raided all the food for themselves.

I heard that from the guy who came to pump the Porta Potties, who'd heard it from I don't know who. A middle-aged man with an unpleasant job, he seemed like the happiest person there—happy, he declared, to be able to make the days more bearable for all these "beautiful" kids who reminded him of his own children. "My son's in Vietnam," he said proudly, probably unaware that many of these kids who reminded him of his children believed that his son was a baby killer, and that there'd be peace in the world if only the American military would come home—so they could drop food and rock stars from helicopters.

People were screaming, "Acid, get your acid here; a buck a tab." And, "Pot, I've got pot, Mexican, ten bucks a lid."

People were making love in the mud and in the bushes and in the open, and one time I found a couple doing it on my tractor.

People were crazy, and I couldn't tell if they were ever going to get their sanity back. Or whether I would. The idea of sanity itself even began to seem insane, like how the mental patients became the rational thinkers in the cult movie *King of Hearts.*

The sanest thing I heard for several days was that the Grateful Dead, Janis Joplin, and the Who wouldn't go onstage and play Saturday night without cash in hand. Their managers had figured out that without gate receipts to deposit Monday morning, every one of those checks written by the Woodstock guys was going to bounce. Wisely—in fact, sanely—the Woodstock partners decided to somehow borrow or steal the cash, because if they didn't, they knew that there would've been a riot to make the Democratic National Convention in Chicago a year before seem like a bar fight. (Another tractor driver told me he'd overheard the conversation, and said the promoters should've just called the musicians' bluff by saying, "Okay, don't play"—but then not let the groups out of there on the helicopters. Good thing he wasn't the promoter. Woodstock would've turned into Jonestown.)

When the Who went on, Abbie Hoffman jumped up on stage and grabbed the mic from Roger Daltrey to yell something political. He'd been tripping for days, hallucinating that someone with a knife was following him. Peter Townshend simultaneously ended Hoffman's bad trip and moment on stage by pistol whipping him with his guitar. Those English, they don't take any cosmic crap.

Sunday broke sunny and much of the crowd started leaving early. They'd had enough of everything and too much of most things. But the parking areas were like one of those puzzles where you have to manipulate the fifteen numbered tiles sequentially. Their cars had become so many pickup sticks, most of them stuck in the mud. I spent the day, and the next day, and the one after that pulling them out, one by one, with my John Deere. They'd see me coming their way and start cheering—John Wayne leading the cavalry to the rescue.

Maybe half the people tipped me, either a buck or so, or a joint or a pill of some kind that I put in my pocket without thinking too much. By Wednesday there were no cars left to pull out, but there were still hundreds of tons of debris—sleeping bags, jackets, backpacks, hats, umbrellas, shoes—just left to rot in the muck. We tractor guys had to gather it all for disposal, which we did after cherry-picking the stuff that could be salvaged with a washing or three. After all, anyone driving a tractor at Woodstock for two bucks an hour probably didn't have a daddy who'd buy him a new North Face sleeping bag to replace the one that had gotten dirty at a rock festival.

My buddy Dale and I couldn't remember the last time we'd slept or where or much about the last week. We slid off our tractors, leaned against a rock wall, spread out our booty haul, and watched the sun set. No music, no motors, no screaming. Never had quiet sounded so good, and I suddenly remembered that this kind of quiet was what I'd set out to hear by backpacking in the Canadian Rockies all those weeks ago.

I emptied my pockets of the tips I'd received, and Dale did too. We separated them into piles—things you smoke, things you swallow, things you rub into your scalp—then selected what we wanted to ingest by color, not knowing what any of them did. Utterly without fear (or intelligence), each of us swallowed a small handful with a swig of canteen water. That's how it was done, back when you knew people's hearts were pure: whatever they gave you was a ticket to paradise.

Dale and I looked at each other and began laughing. We were both so filthy our mothers wouldn't have recognized us, and both so spent we laughed harder at not having the energy to laugh. We laughed at what we'd done these last couple of weeks and seen these last few days—and the next thing I knew a farmer drove up in his old red pickup.

"You boys all right?" he asked.

"Sure, why?"

"Because you've been sitting on that wall for three days now."

That was the last time I ever sat on a wall, so to speak.

And thirty-five years later, I turned to the John Deere executive who'd asked me that simple question. "Oh, yeah, " I said. "I've driven a tractor before."

SORRY I RUINED THE WORLD

★ ★ ★

The Annin flag factory in Oaks, Pennsylvania, is only a few miles from Valley Forge, where Washington camped with his troops during the brutal winter of 1777–1778, so it's a good place to let your mind ponder a little American history, past and present. Oh, and future—fingers crossed.

Back in the good old days, before inmates ran the asylum, I remember Flag Day being a celebration of the American flag, with the date of June 14 marking the anniversary of when it first became our nation's symbol. I happen to know that because we learned it in school, even though the semester usually ended before then; and we observed it by, at the least, flying Old Glory at home or attaching mini versions to our bikes.

These days, however, adherence to Flag Day's roots and aims, at least in some public schools, is considered ugly and jingoistic. Every year you read about some teacher or principal who believes that this holiday is a good excuse to further multiculturalism, by flying or displaying flags of many countries. Just not ours.

Meanwhile, Presidents' Day has become an excuse for a three-day mattress sale, which is offensive to a lot of people like me who remember well when there was no Presidents' Day, per se. Back when, we celebrated two different days, the birthdays of men without whom there would be no America as we know it—or used to know it: Abraham Lincoln, born February 12, and George Washington, born February 22. And the commemorations were held on precisely those days, with newspapers and television running feature stories, and students learning what made them great. No more. Sadly, too many kids no longer learn pride in their country.

There's an infection in the body of America, a virus that makes vast swaths of the populace feel that our country's continuing greatness as the world's only superpower is not only a mistake, but a danger that has to be stopped.

If you think that's a paranoid exaggeration, how else do you account for the constant complaints that the Founding Fathers' remarkable accomplishments are far less important than their status as slaveholders, or that Columbus was not the greatest explorer of all time but rather a genocidal maniac and ecological A-bomb?

How else do you account for the dearth of news coverage about the first free election in Afghanistan's history? It should've been the news story of 2005—usurped only by the first free elections in Iraq. Instead, both were mostly treated with yawns.

How else do you account for liberal commentators like Frank Rich of the *New York Times* slamming Fox News for using the American flag as an onscreen logo—though his own newspaper used to refer to America as "us" and the troops as "our guys" during World War II?

How else do you account for school districts, like the one in Newton, Massachusetts, that believe teaching mathematics is less important than "teaching respect for human differences" by "demonstrating antiracist/antibias behaviors"? What they're actually teaching, of course, is anti-Americanism. As one Newton parent told her local newspaper, "My children do not know Christopher Columbus, except that he was a racist who caused the death of many innocents, or the founders of the nation. They have hardly heard of George Washington or Abraham Lincoln, even though we live in the area that began it all. What they *do* know about are the wonders of Ghana, Mexico, and China."

Our silly educational emphasis on multiculturalism, as opposed to multi-ethnicity, only causes people to be hyperaware of color instead of being color-blind. Back in Bridgeport when I was coming of age, we were as racially and ethnically mixed as it gets—and everybody got along just fine, thank you. That's because we hadn't yet had our consciousness raised enough to know that we should think along racial and ethnic lines.

The fact is that, in another generation, at least half of all native-born Americans won't have learned patriotism even by osmosis. And that's a problem because structures and organizations, even countries, can't survive forever on momentum. They need to be resupplied with energy, and that energy comes from asking not what your country can do for you, but what you can do for your country. In his inaugural address, John F. Kennedy merely put words to the principle on which this country had always operated.

The virus that's infecting America, and that has to be stopped before it kills us all, is self-loathing. And the mad scientists who created it—and swallowed it with the same kind of Kool-Aid that did in the followers of Jim Jones—were Baby Boomers. Today, thanks to my generation—the Woodstock generation—America has a different mentality than it used to. Now, no good deed goes unpunished. We don't ask what we can do for our country. Instead, we demand and insist that our country do everything for us. Rights, not obligations—*that's* the mantra. Legality, not morality—that's the mind-set.

About forty years ago, as we were coming of age, Baby Boomers like me decided to be a "counterculture," which of course meant that we had to "counter" whatever came before, regardless of its merit or intention. So if *they*—our elders—were for it, we were against it. That made us, apparently, the first generation molded in the image of a movie character—Marlon Brando's motorcycle rat in *The Wild One*.

"What're you rebelling against?" he was asked.

"Whaddya got?" he responded.

What we were especially against was anything that got in the way of our doing anything we wanted—like rules. Unless, of course, we made them. And since there were more of us than there were of them (Baby Boomers being history's most populous generation), we wrote or rewrote nearly every rule except the law of gravity. Or thought we did, anyway. Just as we thought we did everything first.

Indeed, it took Boomers to point out the truth that not even the so-called Greatest Generation had the insight to coin—that war is not healthy for children and other living beings.

It took us to question authority (though given how little respect we showed our parents, that was no big leap).

It took us to grant power to "the people"—the addition of "the" thereby elevating a hundred-year-old concept to sublimity by referring only and specifically to the crowds present at antiwar rallies.

It took us to realize that nothing on television is unimportant and that anything not on television can't possibly be important—both of which we realized by watching ourselves grow up on television.

It took us to abolish honorifics like "Mister," which made it okay for our kids' friends to say to us, "Wassup, Dude?" and for everyone to feel really, really good about it.

It took us to bully the college administration into instituting pass-fail (because competition was so, so wrong and led to things like wars and poverty), and us to then transform nursery schools into preschools with admission requirements and astronomical tuition that doom our children to a lifetime of failure if, God forbid, they don't qualify.

It took us to free our black brothers and sisters from four centuries of oppression—not by marching in Selma or becoming Freedom Riders (we were, after all, too young), but through far more subversive and effective means: by buying a hundred million Motown records.

And yes, it took us to bring the F word into common, unashamed, mixed-company usage (as in, "We don't want your f---ing war!" "What the f--- are you doing in my seat?" And, "I'm warning you, don't f--- with me, Mom.").

This was, it can be said, a particularly proud achievement in that it overturned five thousand years of recorded tyranny. Most of us old enough to have been conscious at Woodstock (I say "old enough"—because no one who was actually there was actually conscious) clearly recall being assaulted in the early '60s by cries of "golly" and "swell" and "keen" in the malt shop. We'll never forget how radio programmers across America refused to play Jimmy Dean's "Big Bad John" until he rerecorded its final words to say a "big, big man" instead of "one hell of a man."

And we shake our heads at the sad memory of Art Garfunkel recounting for an early Simon & Garfunkel audience how he and his partner had unwittingly posed for photos against a subway wall on which someone had scribbled, ahem, "the old familiar suggestion." To us, such compulsory euphemisms brought to mind the horrors of medieval France.

Keeping it real—that was the goal. And with mission accomplished, we now sleep soundly after hearing our nine-year-olds keeping it real at dinner.

We didn't mean to ruin the world. It happened by accident. From what I remember, we set out to save the world and make it perfect for children and other living beings. But things ended up pretty much the way they did when I was three and decided my pet parakeet Otto looked cold and covered him with a blanket—or when I surprised Mom by defrosting her ice-caked freezer with a hammer and screwdriver. Surprise! (The pediatrician insisted that the Freon wouldn't do any lasting damage to my brain.) If nothing else, we've proved that old line about the road to hell's paving stones.

What you have to understand is that back in the '60s, everybody who was anybody agreed that America and the world needed saving. Badly. That corny Norman Rockwell USA rah rah rah crap—we considered it the root cause of war and racism and crime and poverty and misery, and we took it as a personal challenge to jackhammer the whole foundation on which the superstition of religion had created the doctrine of oppression that was murdering millions of yellow men in Southeast Asia. (Or something like that.)

So we showed our parents how right Dylan was when he said that their sons and daughters were beyond their command.

Then we followed Tim Leary's prescription to turn on, tune in, and drop out. (He was, after all, a doctor.)

Doing that made it easy to not worry and be happy, as Meher Baba insisted, which of course led to the Maharishi and Baba Ram Dass's teachings that all of life's answers were already inside us. Boy, were they ever. We were founts of eternal knowingness, entitled to everything we ever wanted—born to greatness and superiority, and put here on earth to remake the planet in our perfect image.

That all seemed entirely possible after Woodstock, when the legend became fact almost overnight. Utopia, we insisted, was at hand: the end of war, hate, racism, competition, even work itself. So we adopted an imagined moral legitimacy that we swung as a weapon, believing we were the Adams and Eves of a new order that would usher in the kind of world Rousseau painted. Woodstock was the mount from which we preached about whatever it was that we demanded. We were the "Woodstock Nation" now, and up yours if you didn't like it.

Us against them—that's where we drew the line. We were right, they were wrong, and that was that.

Amazingly, "they" played along with it. These people who'd faced down poverty and evil in the space of fifteen years—they were no match for Woodstock Nation. We convinced them that they'd been lucky to come of age in a time when the world needed them to take out the garbage and sweep off the porch, and assured them that we would've finished the job in ten years—tops—if we'd had the same opportunity. Greatest generation? Hah! The luckiest, maybe. Some old guy raising his pants leg to show off his USS *Indianapolis* scar was no match for the Woodstock Nation's enemies: the suburbs—a stultifying prison of homogeneity intended to subvert our uniqueness and unfairly curb our sense of entitlement; and Vietnam, that bulwark against Eisenhower's dominoes that was as phony to us as McCarthy's list of Communists.

What we told ourselves was that we did better than any previous generation could have done with such thin material, first by protesting against and then by abandoning both the suburbs and Vietnam as not being in our best interests.

Yes, making the personal political required a kind of genius that, we knew for sure, historians would someday declare unmatched in history. What other generation, for example, had had the balls to trash the dean's office, shut down the university, set fire to the ROTC building—and then hand the dean a list of demands that began with "No reprisals"? Which they agreed to!

Boy, just thinking of what we've done brings out my sarcastic streak. But in truth, there's nothing funny about the sledge hammering we've done as a generation on the pillars of Western Civilization.

Countercultures can't stay counter forever—though God knows we tried. Which, in a nutshell, explains how we've mostly ruined the world. We'd established ourselves as an opposition party—or generation—and then never stopped opposing, even after coming of majority age and assuming majority status. We became the majority in America's elite educational, political, and media institutions, where our influence gives us far too much power to flush civilization's righteous babies down the drain with the bathwater.

Too few of us stop to accept the objective, inarguable truth that much of what we opposed actually deserves our support, not contempt. I'd like to hand out to every aging Woodstock Nation member a bumper sticker I once saw: "If you can't change your mind, are you sure you still have one?"

Like baby ducklings imprinting early experiences, we seem to believe that every war is Vietnam—and therefore nothing is worth fighting for. "War is not the answer," says a common bumper sticker, though it never states the question.

Forgotten is that JFK, our childhood hero who defined idealism and optimism for us, got into Vietnam on the premise that America ought to "pay any price, bear any burden . . . in order to assure the survival and the success of liberty." When he died, we decided that only the pursuit of profit, never altruism or American ideals or even righteousness, is what causes war. "People not profit," says the bumper sticker. "No war for oil," is the chant at every antiwar demonstration.

So why do we pay so little attention to wars in which Americans don't fight? After all, those are the ones that tend to be, well, genocidal. For more than seventy years, there hasn't been an antiwar demonstration anywhere in the world unless America was a combatant in the fighting. Startling, no? And in every case the demonstrations, no matter where they were, opposed America's involvement. No surprise, right?

But now comes the ultimate shame and irony: the young Americans who'd banded together by the tens of millions to force America's withdrawal from Vietnam said absolutely nothing about the fighting in Vietnam after our troops left, when the real slaughter began. Nor did Pol Pot hear a discouraging word when he was planting the killing fields. Nor did the Hutus face the wrath of the "peace movement" when they were dispatching a million Tutsis in Rwanda. Nor did Milosevic watch demonstrators fill the streets of San Francisco and New York when he was slaughtering Muslims in Srebrenica. For that matter, there were no bumper stickers protesting the eight-year Iran-Iraq war that killed millions, or the mass murder of Christians by Arab Muslims in Africa.

The inescapable conclusion is that our opposition to Vietnam was animated not by nobility but by not wanting to get shot (or cut our hair). For most, the demonstrations were like some sort of party, and for many they were foreplay. How easy it was back then to get ten thousand or so good buddies together on the quad when five thousand of them faced possibly being drafted as long as the war raged.

For us, America itself became the enemy. And those heady days became the golden days of a life that somehow seemed empty without something to rebel against—something to give you that communal rush—even after the reason you first began hating the enemy was long forgotten. Like the Hatfields and McCoys.

No wonder Boomer college professors who'd protested the war back then nearly pull their hair out over their pro-war students today, even when the students are actually from that part of the globe, know the players, understand firsthand the evil that's being fought, and believe that democracy is a worthy and noble goal that will one day benefit the entire Islamic world.

No wonder *Nation* columnist Katha Pollitt refused to let her daughter fly the American flag on September 12, even within sight of the still-smoking Twin Towers. She feared that America's (brief) unity would be interpreted as a green light for retaliatory military action—even if that action liberated Afghanistan from its seventh-century patriarchal rule that condemned women to a life she could never have tolerated herself.

No wonder acclaimed novelist Rick Moody wrote that Neil

Young, who wrote the song "Ohio" as a tribute to the Kent State students shot by National Guardsmen, was no longer authentic—was, in fact, an impostor—for composing a tribute to Todd Beamer and the other heroes of Flight 93 who sacrificed their own lives to prevent a fourth plane from becoming a weapon on September 11.

No wonder comments at DemocraticUnderground.com on the day of the first historic vote in Iraq included many like this: "I can't believe the Iraqis are buying into this 'democracy' b---s---." In order for their worldview to prevail, America has to fail. America is their enemy, not Islamo-fascism.

Once upon a time, we of the Woodstock Generation professed to care about democracy and freedom everywhere, which was what, after all, fueled the civil rights movement—just as idealism had led Harry Truman to send Americans to Korea and animated FDR to circumvent Republican isolationists so that he could help Churchill fight Hitler before Pearl Harbor. Now, reading and listening to and watching accounts, it's hard to say what we care about, except, of course, ourselves.

Not all fools are Baby Boomers, and not all Baby Boomers are fools. Obviously. But it was Baby Boomers, like me, who created the incubator of American self-hating that has allowed such abysmal foolishness to multiply so alarmingly. Just as we once deemed Vietnamese Communists authentic and America oppressive, today jihadist suicide murders are too frequently rationalized and evangelical Christians too likely called dangerous. For example, the *New York Times* was quick to defend "artist" Andres Serrano's crucifix in urine, but when Muslims around the world began rioting and protesting, it hid behind "cultural sensitivity" instead of running the Danish newspaper editorial cartoons that had outraged them by depicting Mohammed as a terrorist. So much for defending the First Amendment. Obviously, Christians would be treated with more respect and deference if they burned down a building or two the next time their beliefs are defiled.

Surely, our present state was not what General Washington anticipated as he and his army sat there starving and freezing and dying that miserable winter after a string of defeats that, these days, would get the national media demanding immediate surrender.

Civilizations and countries can withstand the most ferocious attacks from the outside, but no civilization, no country, can survive the rot of self-loathing. God help us if the decay ever reaches critical mass, because then it won't take much more than a sneeze to bring the whole structure down.

Yes, that would be a tragedy—in fact, the ultimate tragedy, because freedom everywhere will be extinguished. Then those who hated America most will discover firsthand how oppressively brutal an enemy can really be . . . when the enemy is not us.

"HISTORY WILL BE KIND TO ME, FOR I INTEND TO WRITE IT"

★   ★   ★

Most people nowadays understand the phrase "left on the cutting room floor," which refers to camera footage taken but not used in the final screen version. In fact, most of what's recorded for movies and TV isn't seen by the viewing public, and that's especially true of *John Ratzenberger's Made in America*. We cover a factory two dozen ways from next Sunday, since we never know until we sit down to put everything together how it's going to go.

One moment from the show's first season that I knew, even as it was happening, would never make it to the screen came after I saw a small poster of Winston Churchill taped to a factory worker's lathe. At the time, American and British troops had just toppled Saddam Hussein's Iraq, and the presumption was that any day we would start to uncover his presumed stockpiles of nuclear, biological, and chemical weapons.

As it happens, Churchill, warts and all, is one of my top three (and the other two change with my moods) favorite historical figures. Maybe I should use the word "character," because that he was. He drank upon waking, smoked incessantly, dictated his (Nobel Prize–winning) writings to a secretary while naked, suffered fools not at all, surgically removed the pretensions from others with his wit, and could fill a book of quotable quotations all by himself. When George Bernard Shaw sent him two tickets to the opening of his new play along with a note that said, "Bring a friend—if you have one," Churchill immediately returned them along with his own note: "Sorry, but I am engaged that evening. Please send tickets for the second night—if you have one."

Then there was the time that Churchill and Lady Astor had been verbally jousting all weekend at Blenheim Castle. At last Lady Astor said, "If I were your wife, I'd put poison in your coffee." To which Churchill replied, "If I were your husband, I'd drink it."

When I stopped to admire the Churchill poster, I said to the guy at the lathe, "Unless this is a dart board, and I don't see any holes in it, I like your taste in heroes."

He smiled and thanked me, then said he kept the Old Bulldog there as a reminder.

"Of what?" I asked.

"That most people are followers, and that's why we need leaders."

Just right.

Most of us aren't just followers; most of us believe that we live outside of history—that the kinds of events we read about in history books won't happen in our lifetimes and therefore be in future history books. And that makes for some dangerous thinking, as it did in Churchill's day.

Every generation, it seems, has to relearn the lessons of history. But we only seem to learn them the hard way—in retrospect. After it's too late. And that's despite everyone's supposed familiarity with the George Santayana quotation about those not remembering history being condemned to repeat it. For most of us, the philosopher's wisdom is just so many words. So it was for our forebears, whom our history books blame for their blindness, just as our children will read about our mistakes someday.

Occasionally, though, someone does get it right ahead of time and has to face the burden of Cassandra, the Greek mythological heroine who could foresee the future but whose warnings were always perceived as foolishness—until they came true. This was the fate of Winston Churchill in the 1930s, and the lesson we would do well to learn from him—the one for which he is justifiably famous—has to do with appeasing aggression and evil.

It's the colossal story of what didn't happen and what did happen before World War II, and it's about two men. The first was idealistic, the second a realist. The first saw what he believed. The second believed what he saw. The first nearly destroyed us; the second helped to save us. The first was Neville Chamberlain, prime minister of Great Britain in the late 1930s. The second was Winston Churchill, who, unlike most of us, didn't require a history book to recognize what he would later call a "gathering storm."

Now, more than seventy years later, at a time when our schools seem to be focusing less on George Washington (unless it's as a slaveholder) and more on Chalchiuhtlicue (the Aztec goddess of running water—but of course you knew that), I think it's critical that if we teach only one moment in history, it should be Churchill's battle to rally the free world against the growing danger of Nazi Germany—for it has the power and truth of parable. And as the events of September 11 made sick-eningly clear, it's more relevant than ever.

The story actually begins in the wake of World War I. Millions had died. Millions more had lost their souls.

For the British, who'd fought on the winning side, the war had been such a horrific and searing experience that most people no longer believed that anything—not freedom, not even England itself—was worth dying or even fighting for. Hundreds of thousands of England's brightest young men lined up to sign pledges that they would never again fight to defend king and country.

For the Germans, the war had meant not only the shame of defeat but also economic ruin. To lead them out of despair and anger, they turned to a charismatic demagogue, Adolf Hitler. And lead them he did—toward another war.

That this was his direction is obvious to all of us who have the benefit of history. In those days, however, the Western world was still hung over from the fighting and could see only what they'd already chosen to believe. And what they believed was that Hitler's massive rearming of Germany—a violation of the Versailles Treaty ending the war—was meant to reinvigorate the German economy. It wasn't, they insisted, anyone else's business what Germany did inside its own borders.

Pacifism had gripped the British populace like an epidemic fever. Reflecting that, Britain's ruling Labor Party voted down nearly all military spending. At one political rally whose aim was complete British disarmament "as an example to other [countries]," the noted economist Roy Harrod, who was then in his thirties, asked one of the enthusiastic young pacifists whether he truly believed that England's example would inspire Hitler and Mussolini to disarm too. "Oh, Roy," the young man moaned. "Have you lost all your idealism?"

It had been a while since Churchill lost his idealism. To him, idealism and pacifism were not the -isms of serious adults responsible for guarding freedom and liberty, because he could see the virulent menace to both forming on the continent. A student and scholar of history, especially military history, Churchill had no reason to doubt Hitler's direction. He had, after all, read *Mein Kampf;* and through his own network of contacts he could reliably report the alarming buildup of the German air force and army. As early as 1929, before Hitler even became Germany's chancellor, Churchill said, "If a dog makes a dash for my trousers, I shoot him down before he can bite."

Throughout the 1930s, Churchill warned repeatedly that war was inevitable, just as it had been in the years prior to World War I, when Germany was building up its navy to unprecedented strength. Then, as First Lord of the Admiralty, Churchill had been charged with making England's navy equally formidable. But now, in his sixties and a member of Parliament holding no cabinet position, he was considered old, impotent, cranky, and out of date.

In 1935, Britain and France ignored Hitler's reinstatement of a military draft (with a target of building the largest army on earth: 550,000 strong), which also violated the Treaty of Versailles. And then a year later, they rationalized yet another violation when Hitler made a pact with Mussolini. Churchill could see that England's and France's inaction was emboldening Hitler by the day, and warned again that war would be inescapable unless England acted immediately to counter the growing threat by rebuilding its armed forces. When he claimed that Hitler had dark plans for the continent of Europe and, indeed, the world, he was laughed at or ignored. After all, Hitler kept telling the democracies exactly what he knew they wanted to hear. "Germany wants peace," he declared in a speech at the Reichstag, introducing his own thirteen-point "peace" program. "None of us," he promised, "means to threaten anyone."

Churchill looked at Hitler's actions, not at his words, but the ruling elite and the press preferred those sweet promises even as they belied the deeds.

Rarely has a man of prominence been so out of touch with his times as Churchill was, and that is probably how history would have remembered him, if it remembered him at all, had not France committed a blunder of colossal—no, immeasurable—proportions in March of 1936. That was when Hitler sent three ragtag battalions—many on horseback!—to reoccupy the Rhineland, an industrial area between Germany and France that the Treaty of Versailles prohibited Hitler from occupying. Their orders were to retreat if the French—who, like the British, were actually obliged by two treaties to defend the Rhineland—offered even a pistol's worth of resistance. Though France had the largest army in the world at the time, half a million strong, the French generals refused to act. Too bad. Historians now agree that the battle, if there had been one, would've ended quickly and been decisive.

Hitler later called those days the most nerve-wracking of his life (presumably until he had to choose a form of suicide), and admitted that his rise would likely have ended had the French reacted with force. But now he could see that there was no one to stop him.

Unlike Churchill, Neville Chamberlain was a man perfectly suited to the British (and French) mood, taking office as prime minister in 1937 (after serving as Chancellor of the Exchequer) on a pacifist platform. Like most of his countrymen, he disregarded the news from Germany about the subjugation of Jews and intellectuals. He scoffed at reports, both from his own government and from Churchill, that Germany was planning to invade its neighbors, starting with Austria. He chose not to believe anything he didn't want to hear. What he shared with his philosophical compatriot across the pond, Joseph Kennedy, was the attitude of a businessman (which he'd been before entering politics) who considered war a needless expense.

In 1938, Hitler amassed troops along the Austrian border and then absorbed that country into what he now named the Third Reich. It was yet another violation of Versailles—and still Chamberlain carried on with the kind of politically correct thinking that sounds today so unfortunately modern. "It has always seemed to me," he told Parliament, "that in dealing with foreign countries, we do not give ourselves a chance of success unless we try to understand their mentality, which is not always the same as our own. And it really is astonishing to contemplate how the identically same facts are regarded from two different angles." (Today we talk about "root causes.")

Churchill was appalled, but without power he could only continue to issue his dire warnings.

Anyway, you know the rest. Hitler demanded that Czechoslovakia become a part of greater Germany, threatening war if he couldn't "legally" take the country. This led to the infamous Munich Pact, where a delegation led by Chamberlain sold out Czechoslovakia to Germany in exchange for a promise from Hitler that his territorial grabs would stop there. Returning to

England, Chamberlain appeared before cheering throngs, declared that he had achieved "peace for our time," and told them to "Go home and get a nice quiet sleep." As if they weren't already. Now more than ever, Churchill's was a lone voice of doom.

"Do not suppose," he told the House of Commons, "that this is the end. It is only the beginning of the reckoning. This is only the first sip, the first taste of a bitter cup that will be proffered to us year by year unless, by a supreme recovery of moral health and martial vigor, we arise again and take our stand for freedom as in the olden time."

His Cassandra warnings ignored, a year later Germany invaded Poland, and the second "war to end all wars" began in earnest.

Chamberlain spoke to his nation: "No man can say that the government could have done more to try to keep open the way for an honorable and equitable settlement of the dispute between Germany and Poland. Nor have we neglected any means of making it crystal clear to the German government that if they insisted on using force again in the manner in which they had used it in the past we were resolved to oppose them by force." Of course, Chamberlain had done precisely the opposite of what he claimed, by showing Hitler time and again that his violence would be met with indifference. And by now the rest of England knew it, too. Chamberlain soon resigned, and the new prime minister, Winston Churchill, led the British to their finest hour.

By the time World War II ended, more than 50 million people had died, which was about 50 million more than necessary.

But the truth, then as now, is that good people are slow to accept that evil people exist—and that they cannot be reasoned with or made to see the error of their ways by appealing to the better angels of their nature. To us—the products of a liberal, enlightened tradition—the idea of reacting aggressively to aggression seems unenlightened and illiberal. No matter that playground bullies are almost always stopped by violence. We choose to think that geopolitics need not play by the same crude rules. But whether they're the meanest kid on the block or the shrewdest dictator on the continent, aggressors are always emboldened by the inaction of their victims and witnesses to their crimes. They interpret inaction as a green light to escalation.

And that brings us to September 11 and the war on terror, which is actually a war—political correctness aside—on a form of fascism potentially more terrifying, destructive, and intractable than Nazism, because its adherents glorify their own deaths to achieve a world governed by fundamentalist Islamic law (*sharia*). In the words of al-Qaeda's leader in Iraq, Abu Musab al-Zarqawi, "The attacks will not cease until after the victory of Islam and the setting up of *sharia* . . . on the entire earth." This is why we fight—not to impose democracy on Iraq or another country because we want everyone to live as we do; but because they want to impose their way of life on *us*, just as Hitler did.

Sadly, we are to blame for letting the Islamic fascist movement become bigger than most of us want to admit, and fewer still of us want to do anything about.

The same Islamo-fascism that was behind the storming of the American embassy in Tehran, and the taking of fifty-two American hostages for 444 days in 1979, was also behind the blowing up of our Marine barracks in Beirut, Lebanon, which killed 241 Americans in 1983; the attempted toppling of the

World Trade Center that killed six and wounded hundreds in 1993; the blowing up of the Khobar Towers barracks in Saudi Arabia that killed nineteen Americans and wounded hundreds in 1996; the blowing up of two American embassies in Africa, which killed hundreds in 1998; and the blowing up of the USS *Cole*, which killed seventeen sailors and wounded dozens in the waters off Yemen in 2000.

For none of those acts were the perpetrators or the Islamic groups behind them punished, except for some misguided and largely symbolic cruise missiles that only served to embolden the terrorists by making the United States appear to be, in the words of Osama bin Laden, a paper tiger. So it's no wonder that he and his cohorts came to believe that the United States would offer little more than a limp response to September 11.

Now they know better. And so should we.

But do we? I'm not sure.

The calls for immediate withdrawal from Iraq, disregarding the almost certain consequences; the furor over wiretapping terrorists' phone calls; the mantra of "Bush lied"; the constant focus on the number of soldiers' deaths—these are all signs that we are not serious about winning for the same reason that Chamberlain's England turned deaf and blind after World War I: because we believe in fairy tales. Just as England and France did nothing while Germany was rearming and invading other territories, we did nothing while we were attacked for more than two decades.

Just look at the outcome: doing nothing did nothing to appease our enemies, whom we were slow to call enemies despite their repeated attacks and declarations of war. And yet a great many people want us to more or less do nothing again, by opposing our military's fighting to replace dictatorial fascism with at least a workable form of democracy. Sometimes I can barely unravel the ironies of their thinking, as when Barbra Streisand grumbled about the first free elections in the history of the Arab world: "The result of the December election," she wrote, "has plunged Iraq into political turmoil."

The most adamant and vicious critics of the fighting seem to have two main complaints (to put it mildly). The first is that President Bush invaded Iraq "illegally"—that is, without a blessing from the United Nations; and the second is that he didn't find the weapons of mass destruction that were supposed to be there. As it happens, the two reasons are intertwined.

The United Nations was created in the ashes of World War II by leaders who imagined that all countries had had the fight knocked out of them forever, and that every country now wanted nothing more than to live in peace and just needed a place to talk out any disagreements. It was a fiction then and it's a fiction now, when fewer than half of UN member countries are democracies and the rest range from repressive dictator-ships to cults of personality to one-party governments to thugocracies to Islamic theocracies. In fact, nearly a third of member states are now entirely or majority Muslim countries with an inherently different agenda to enact than the UN's mission statement, recorded in the Universal Declaration of Human Rights and applicable to all member states. (Article 18, for example: "Everyone has the right to freedom of thought, conscience and religion; this right includes freedom to change his religion or belief, and freedom, either alone or in commu-nity with others and in public or private, to manifest his religion or belief in teaching, practice, worship and observance.") So the UN's inherent moral legitimacy is, at the least, open to earnest analysis.

While the historical truth is that democracies generally do not war against each other, the UN does not even encourage, let alone insist, that its members begin to move toward democratization. In the past two decades, resolutions condemning democratic Israel are passed with nauseating regularity (having been sponsored by Israel's dictatorial enemies), while true tyrants are often coddled and praised. In Zimbabwe, for example, Robert Mugabe is literally destroying his country through corruption, forced eviction of white farmers whose crops feed the people, and by demolishing white-owned businesses and factories that employ thousands. But French president Jacques Chirac (who derisively called President Bush a "cowboy") has received him as an honored guest. Meanwhile, fascist dictatorships like Syria (one of the few countries our own State Department designates as a purveyor of terrorism) are elected to serve on the powerful Security Council. Less than a month after 9/11, the vote for Syria in the General Assembly was 160 to 18. That sure sounds like a message to me, but one that not enough of us care to hear for what it says.

Those who believe that only the United Nations can legitimately determine when we do or do not go to war should keep in mind that the UN was adamantly against doing anything to stop the ethnic cleansing in Yugoslavia—and in fact meekly allowed the slaughter of 1,700 Muslim men in the supposed "safe haven" of Srebrenica set up by the UN when its "peace-keepers" stepped aside and let the Serb murderers in. (By the way, President Clinton's seventy-eight-day bombing campaign in Kosovo—a "moral imperative," he correctly said—was carried out *without* UN approval.)

As for Rwanda, the genocide of nearly a million Tutsis by Hutus was essentially encouraged by the UN, which commanded its troops on the ground to stand by and do nothing when, like Germany in the Rhineland, they could've easily stopped the aggressors with a few well-placed shots. It's disgusting—more so when you consider that the UN official who gave the order to do nothing was Kofi Annan, the current secretary general.

The romantic view that millions have of the United Nations and its authority to declare a "just" war should know that in its sixty-year history, the UN has given its blessing to only two conflicts: the Korean War and the first Gulf War. The first is technically still ongoing, more than fifty-five years later, with only a ceasefire instead of a negotiated peace treaty in place. And the second was still technically ongoing, twelve years after its supposed end, when we invaded Iraq. Saddam Hussein had just defied the seventeenth UN resolution aimed at forcing him to comply with the terms of the ceasefire that had kept him in power since 1991. All he had to do to stay in power and avoid invasion was prove that he had indeed disarmed his weapons of mass destruction—something, by the way, he was supposed to have done fifteen days after signing that ceasefire.

Fifteen days. Twelve years ago.

When is enough enough? That's the question all those who champion the United Nations and lament America's end-run into Iraq ought to ask themselves. Because the sum of those unobserved resolutions had the effect of making the United Nations irrelevant, like an ineffectual parent who keeps escalating the threat of punishment but never takes action. "I'm warning you . . . I'm really warning you . . . You do that one more time and you're gonna get it . . . What did I tell you? Don't you dare do that again . . . Boy, are you asking for it. . . ." To some degree, the United States restored the UN's significance by saving it from an eighteenth resolution. Then a nineteenth. And so on.

What's interesting to me is that the same people who claim we went to war in Iraq so that Dick Cheney could enrich his buddies at Halliburton apparently see no conflict of interest at the UN, where Security Council members Russia and France were both chest deep in business with Saddam's Iraq, meaning that they were bound to veto any war resolution anyway in order to protect their own multibillion-dollar skim. Before the invasion, France rejected President Bush's last compromise offer to Iraq even *before* Saddam Hussein did.

What those who believe in peace at any price don't understand is that their attitude always leaves it to the aggressor to determine the terms of peace. A bumper sticker I see often says, "You cannot simultaneously prevent and prepare for war." The line is attributed to Einstein, but it's sheer nonsense. The only way you *can* prevent war is by preparing for it—as Churchill tried to warn us.

Conversely, the French, the Russians, the Germans, and every protester in this country all but insured that there *would* be a war by leading Saddam Hussein to conclude that the leaders of democratic countries would not act against their own people's wishes for peace, which were the only wishes he could see being televised around the world at rallies. He figured he had only to hold on a little longer, all the while continuing to hand out those billions of oil dollars that were supposed to go for Iraqi food and medicine but that were instead finding their way to the UN, to French and Russian and German officials, and to his own Swiss bank accounts.

I have no doubt that many—maybe even most, but certainly not all—antiwar protesters sincerely want the fighting to end and the good guys to win. But they should understand that if there is one lesson to be learned from Vietnam, it is that protests in this country embolden the enemy. (So does calling terrorists "freedom fighters," a term used admiringly by both Cindy Sheehan and Michael Moore.) As the North Vietnamese general Vo Nguyen Giap later admitted, he could never beat us on the battlefield—but he knew he didn't have to; watching the news every day encouraged him to hang on until we couldn't.

Don't think for a moment that the so-called insurgents in Iraq didn't also learn the lessons of Vietnam and haven't themselves also come to believe that it's only a matter of time before we civilians force our politicians to order our troops home before the mission is complete. They must laugh themselves silly when they see speakers representing feminist groups like the National Organization for Women calling for immediate withdrawal at antiwar rallies, or when Queers for Palestine (no kidding), a gay political group, marches with placards that say "Palestine is still the issue." The closest parallel I can think of to describe the irony of their positions would be cows rooting for the butcher.

Apparently, NOW and Queers for Palestine have missed the stakes here: preservation of our free and tolerant societies that protect the rights of, among others, women and gays. Strict Islamic societies treat women essentially as slaves—the property of men. In Taliban-led Afghanistan, for example, women were prohibited from working and learning to read, and were frequently beaten, whipped, subjected to amputations, and beheaded for infractions like an inch of ankle showing from under the burka. Knowing that, feminists in pre-war days used to express solidarity with their Afghani "sisters," though they later opposed taking the steps that actually freed them.

All over the Muslim world, women are murdered with impunity for the crime (yes, the victim's crime) of being raped. Fathers slit their daughters' throats for having boyfriends. Husbands beat their wives to death for not pleasing them sexually—or *for* pleasing them sexually; it's a whim. Brothers strangle their sisters for bringing "dishonor" to the family. In Saudi Arabia a few years ago, fifteen schoolgirls were burned to death after they were prevented from fleeing their burning school because they weren't dressed properly in headscarves and black robes. And such crimes take place in the *West*, too—England, France, Holland, Canada—wherever authorities are loathe to prosecute the offenders for fear of appearing culturally insensitive to the issue of "honor killings." Yet, NOW actually urged the same Iraqi women who'd been subject to Saddam's official rape rooms "to think twice before accepting" their new constitution—a constitution that reserved a minimum percentage of elected offices for women.

Meanwhile, Queers for Palestine insists that Israel vacate so-called Palestinian lands. Nothing, literally nothing, better illustrates the West's suicidal ignorance. As Sheikh Khalid Yasin—a former *Christian*—once observed coolly, "The sharia is very clear about it, the punishment for homosexuality, bestiality or anything like that is death. We don't make any excuses about that, it's not our law—it's the Koran."

In areas where the Koran is observed—like the one that the

politically correct have begun calling "Palestine"—gays are tortured mercilessly or murdered with impunity, and Islamic clergy debate the best way to execute them: hanging, pushing from the top of a tall building, having a brick wall collapse on them, stoning, and so on.

A few years ago, the liberal *New Republic* magazine published a report from Israel about a twenty-one-year-old gay Palestinian who was beaten by his family, then arrested and hung "by his arms from the ceiling," then "forced to stand in sewage water up to his neck, his head covered by a sack filled with feces, and then he was thrown into a dark cell infested with insects and other creatures he could feel but not see. . . . During one interrogation, police stripped him and forced him to sit on a Coke bottle. Through the entire ordeal he was taunted by interrogators, jailers, and fellow prisoners for being a homosexual.

"When he was released a few months later, Tayseer crossed into Israel. He now lives illegally in an Arab Israeli village and works in a restaurant. His dream is to move to Tel Aviv. 'No one there cares if you're gay,' he says." (For the benefit of Queers for Palestine members, who apparently don't know better: Tel Aviv is in Israel.)

The story went on to describe other atrocities against gays for no crime other than their sexuality, like a man thrown into a pit without food and water and left to die, which he did— slowly and in agony, as people watched and cheered. There are hundreds and thousands of other documented stories like these. Too bad Queers for Palestine doesn't understand that in the war being fought by the other side—the side they're rooting for—they themselves are the highest-value targets.

But we, too, root for the enemy when we ignorantly claim

that the war is phony, or that it's "over there" and not coming to these shores. Because it's real and already did.

Churchill had Hitler pegged, and though Saddam Hussein was certainly no Hitler, he would've been vastly more powerful than Hitler if he had ever been allowed to develop nuclear weapons. That we didn't find any isn't bad news or cause for breast beating; it's good news that we evidently kept him from something terrible.

The real bad news is that the political fallout from failing to find these weapons may weaken the will of our leaders to do something about the gathering storm in Iran, which has been playing the same listen-to-what-I-say-not-what-I-do game with the European Union and the International Atomic Energy Agency that Hitler did with France and England. God help us all if that Islamic theocracy, which believes only and entirely in *sharia*, succeeds in developing nuclear weapons. Like Hitler in *Mein Kampf*, Iranian President Mahmoud Ahmadinejad has flatly and unashamedly declared his intentions: wiping Israel off the map, something that Israel would object to with weapons in kind, thus bringing on a conflagration too terrible to contemplate; and spreading seventh-century Islam across the continents. This is the type of Islam in which teenage girls are hanged in public for "committing acts incompatible with chastity," that is, being raped.

"We must prepare ourselves," said Ahmadinejad, who unabashedly believes in the apocalypse and in provoking it, "to rule the world."

We in the West ignore his bluster, his ambitions, and his developing weapons at our own peril, just as we did Hitler's in the 1930s.

If France had stopped Germany in the Rhineland, nothing,

happily, would have been the same, and Churchill would now be a footnote—the crackpot who kept warning of a war that never came. Who would know that he wasn't wrong?

My friend at the factory with the Churchill poster had it right, that most people are followers and that's why we need leaders—to save us from our ignorance and to do the right thing, even when history won't record that by doing so, they kept us from annihilation.

The best scenes, sometimes, are left on the cutting room floor.

THE MORALLY STUPID

★　★　★

When I was a kid, the smartest man around was a gas station operator, Mr. Sloane. The guy knew everything there was to know—or so it seemed to me, someone who knew little. Sometimes I'd go there just to hang out with him and hear his fascinating stories about Abraham Lincoln or the Peloponnesian Wars or Isaac Newton's apple. He had a story for every occasion, each more fascinating than the last. One time I asked him how he knew all this stuff. "Did you go to college or something?"

It's not as silly a question as it might seem today; at the time I'd never met anyone who'd gone to college, so I had no idea what the typical grad did or didn't know. On the other hand, I probably should've been a little quicker on the uptake and made a connection between what he told me and the shelves full of books against the walls in the small office area where he'd sit and read every spare second between pumping gas and tuning a Chevy 327. He'd groan at having to put down his book or interrupt a story when someone's front wheels drove over the black cable that squeezed a dong inside to announce the arrival.

He laughed at the question and confined himself to only a hint of sarcasm, aware that college graduates were as rare in our part of the world as four-leaf clovers. "It's amazing, John, what you can find in a book. *This* is my college," he said. "This library and the one at home."

I'm not sure what happened to Mr. Sloane. One day he was at the station, the next he was gone—and so were his books; the shelves were mostly empty, except for a few greasy parts catalogs. Over the years, I've thought of him a hundred times, because he's remained my personal model of what smart people should be. Sure, there's probably some rose coloring added to my childhood memories, but I don't believe Mr. Sloane suffered an exalted sense of his own importance at knowing what he knew, unlike so many brilliant people I've met. Like most autodidacts, he never equated knowledge with wisdom or confused smarts with goodness.

The last time I had occasion to wonder what old Mr. Sloane would think came when I was reading the newspaper in my hotel room one morning before going to a factory in San Francisco. There was a story about the then-imminent selection of the jury for Michael Jackson's molestation trial: "Legal experts say prosecutors will look for jurors who are older, conservative, less taken with celebrity, willing to accept authority, and appalled by child molestation. Jackson's attorneys may look for more liberal jurors who have advanced degrees and are critical thinkers who question authority."

These are fairly startling statements. The idea that liberals might be less appalled by child molestation—or keep an open mind about it—is to me like debris in my food that won't go down. And I won't try to make it go.

So what got me thinking about the good old days in that gas station was the notion that people with advanced degrees, like the kind I once imagined Mr. Sloane to have, would be less appalled by heinous behavior. That doesn't say good things about our concept of what it means to be intelligent today.

A few years ago a sixteen-year-old boy driving a new Lincoln coupe at 70 mph—twice the speed limit—careened off a hillside and hit the car carrying my good buddy's wife and daughter. They were lucky to walk away, and so was the kid.

Later that night his mother told my buddy how surprised she was by his reckless driving. "He got 1550 on his SAT," she cried.

"What do you do for a living?" he asked.

College professor, she told him.

That didn't surprise him. Or me. Like millions of intellectual elites, this lady assumed an inherent connection between intelligence and goodness, and between intelligence and wisdom, as though there exists some objective domain of ethicality to which Mensa members are automatically admitted.

The presumption is obviously wrong, but even so it begins to explain why so many academics and pundits and intelligentsia members delight in ridiculing President Bush's purported lack of gray matter. That he doesn't see the truths they consider self-evident means he must be stupid; and because he is, he can be neither good nor wise—as his policies then self-evidently confirm to them. In this kind of circular logic, the man's staircase never reaches the top floor.

Googling "Bush" and "stupid" yields about 17 million hits,

including countless thousands called, literally, "stupid Bush." There's the "stupid Bush quote of the day," "stupid Bush and his idiot minions," "stupid Bush" parody lyrics to several songs ("Stupid Bush kid, a king who must lie . . ."), and the brilliant assertion that "Bush is just stupid spelled backwards," which must've been composed by someone who thinks Evian spelled backwards is water.

Also available for your pleasure are Photoshopped composites of the president wearing a dunce cap and as Alfred E. Neuman; Cher's opinion that Bush is "stupid" and "lazy"; actor David Clennon's explanation for why the president is no Hitler: "Because George Bush . . . is not as smart as Adolf Hitler"; Oxford University professor Richard Dawkins's verdict that "Bush isn't quite as stupid as he sounds, and heaven knows he can't be as stupid as he looks"; and Fidel Castro's hope that the president not be "as stupid as he seems."

Of course, many of the same millions who call Bush dumb consider Bill Clinton the White House's most brilliant occupant. Googling "Clinton" and "stupid" generates two-thirds fewer hits, and most of those are references to the former president's 1992 campaign signature slogan, "It's the economy, stupid," or variations on it like, "It's the education, stupid" and "It's the lying, stupid." No one, apparently, regards the president who spent half his time in the Oval Office with his pants down as dim-witted.

Which is why few seemed surprised during President Bush's first term when the Lovenstein Institute of Scranton, Pennsylvania, led by Dr. Werner R. Lovenstein and Professor Patricia F. Dilliams, released its study ranking the IQs of every president over the previous fifty years. Foremost among them, with 182, was Bill Clinton, followed in order by Jimmy Carter, John F. Kennedy, Richard Nixon, and Franklin Roosevelt (so much for fifty years).

As for the dumbest chief executives, they were, in descending order, Ronald Reagan, George H. W. Bush, and his son, the current president, whose 91 charted in at exactly half of Clinton's.

The results were so alarming—oy, our president is a complete doofus!—they were forwarded via e-mail tens of millions of times, from one concerned citizen to another, and prompted liberal cartoonist Gary Trudeau to compose a Doonesbury strip around Bush's low "intelligence quota."

Just one problem. There is no Lovenstein Institute, no Dr. Lovenstein, no Professor Dilliams. That the Internet ruse spread so quickly, without anyone bothering to immediately verify the results, explains more about our culture than it does about our president. (I wonder why no one called Trudeau and others like him "stupid" after they fell for the ruse. Actually, no I don't.)

We live in an age when pure intelligence is valued and honored beyond all bounds of reason and logic. There's almost a cult of worship around it, particularly among intellectual elites on the left—those who set the agenda for schools and media. By their books, syllabi, tenure, lectures, speeches, op-eds, public pronouncements, and name-calling criticisms, they have split the world into hemispheres: the intelligent and the unintelligent. The intelligent (and their offspring) now comprise the group that used to be called "our kind of people" in the time when Northeastern WASPs from "the right" families had first dibs on Harvard and Yale. But nowadays it has to be the right kind of intelligence. Brilliant conservatives like, say, Charles Krauthammer and George Will, need not apply for membership, since intelligence and conservatism are considered mutually exclusive; conservatives, by definition, cannot be smart. That's why blue-state elites think of red-staters as being too dumb to know what's in their own best interests.

In some ways, the "right" kind of intelligence is more tyrannical than the old world-at-their-feet arrogance bred in prep schools generations ago. While the upper crust were at least taught manners and noblesse oblige—"It is proper to demand more from the man with exceptional advantages than from the man without them," said Teddy Roosevelt—today's aspiring intelligentsia (especially in the bigger cities) too often learn that bright makes right.

One man I heard about bragged that his nine-year-old son mouths off to camp counselors—"because he's so much smarter than they are." Another man couldn't decide whether he'd prefer his brilliant but tortured son to be happy or accomplished. And a woman watched with pride and nodded approvingly as her *seven-year-old* daughter called an adult stupid for disagreeing with her memorized contention that the president had better things to worry about—"like the economy, duh"—than Iraq.

Our next generation of intellectual elites may not be smarter than the last one, but they're likely to be ruder and more ruthless, given that they're being raised in many cases by new-money parents who turned nursery schools into "preschools" that are harder to get into and cost more than a four-year college used to, and who threaten lawsuits when the school deems junior not smart enough for the gifted-and-talented program.

Intelligence, it seems, is the new Gucci.

The question no one ever seems to ask is this: Intelligence in the service of what?

Answering that question leads back to the president—Carter, that is. As the fictitious Lovenstein Institute pointed out, Jimmy Carter's stellar intellect has become an article of faith. He was a nuclear engineer, also a poet. And yet, this was the man who, in 1979, looked Soviet leader Leonid Brezhnev in the eye, kissed him on both cheeks, proclaimed him a partner in peace . . . and then watched the Soviet Union invade Afghanistan (thus starting World War III, the one we're fighting now). A quarter-century later (around the time Carter kissed Kim Jong Il and returned from Pyongyang, North Korea, proclaiming peace for our time), President Clinton, a man who devoured whole libraries on his vacation, did the same with Palestinian leader Yasser Arafat—and for a decade afterward, Israel paid the price for his belief in the power of his intellect to prevail over irrationality. Rwanda, Somalia, and Srebrenica paid similar prices for their intellectual brilliance and feeble policies.

Maybe Carter and Clinton really were so smart, seeing so many sides of every issue, that what appeared to their eyes was not a unified image but a kind of pixilated version of the big picture that registers trees instead of forest. But was it helpful? Well, judging by some of the results, you'd have to say no. To this day, their considerable intellects persuade them and their admirers of their own righteousness: just as Bush's stupidity ipso facto makes him wrong, their intelligence makes them always right.

"When I was in office," Clinton declared in 2002, "inspections [in Iraq] worked." Huh? Saddam Hussein kicked the weapons inspectors out of Iraq in 1998 and refused them entry again until President Bush began rattling sabers and threatening action. Those four unaccounted-for years were what led the president to believe that Iraq was a dangerous rogue state (and by the way, I still believe that we'll find those weapons of mass destruction in Syria).

More recently, Clinton claimed that, as president, he was "a naïve person who believed in the rule of law." Ditto, huh? This was the only president in the history of the United States convicted of perjury and stripped of his law license. That the matter was related to sex is irrelevant; even presidents are bound by courtroom oaths.

Carter, meanwhile, promoted his recent book by claiming that President Bush manipulated the intelligence on Iraq in order to justify the invasion, which is the same as calling him a liar and an autocrat, indeed a tyrant, when in fact Bush's conclusions were identical to the Clinton administration's. No matter. Carter actually still believes that until Bush became president, the North Koreans honored their pledge to him not to restart their existing nuclear power plant, or reprocess their spent fuel rods to produce weapons-grade plutonium. The truth? Kim Il Sung began rebuilding his nuclear weapons program almost the moment Carter's plane took off.

The frequent comparison of Bush to Hitler by the president's political adversaries serves as an ironic reminder that there is no inherent correlation between intelligence and morality. Intelligence in the service of immorality (Hitler, for example) produces unspeakable evil, while intelligence in the service of idealism (Carter, etc.) often allows evil to fester.

If it were really true that a high IQ in and of itself guaranteed peace and prosperity, then we should hold a contest to determine who has the highest IQ in the country and appoint him or her president right now and be done with democratic elections. But I don't want, say, Professor Stephen Hawking as president, nor any of the other truly brilliant people I know. Sure, it's entertaining to sit at a dinner table and behold gifted minds interacting with other gifted minds, and to hear them get all the *Jeopardy* questions right, and to read and watch and listen to their works of genius. But that's not the same as admiring their character, which is often less developed than their ability to rip someone apart with their wit. Anyway, for all their verbal eloquence and literary finger-pointing, which big issues, exactly, have the reigning intelligentsia been correct about since the '60s? One would be hard-pressed to compose a short list.

The truth, which George Orwell pointed out in his famous remark—"Some ideas are so stupid, only an intellectual could believe them"—is that truly brilliant people and truly talented people often buy into truly unintelligent ideas.

George Bernard Shaw believed in Hitler and Stalin.

Princeton professor of bioethics Peter Singer believes that parents ought to be able to murder their disabled children. Norman Mailer believed that convicted murderer Jack Henry Abbot deserved to be paroled because he could write well (and that we went to war in Iraq to bolster the white-male ego).

Prominent people in Hollywood and publishing argued for California governor Arnold Schwarzenegger to commute the death sentence of Stanley "Tookie" Williams, founder of the notorious Crips street gang, on the grounds that he wrote children's books, which allegedly proved that he'd changed his ways.

The best and the brightest, as we learned from JFK's advisers, offer little protection against absolute foolishness—and may, perhaps, be more susceptible to it, given the anecdotal evidence suggesting that brilliance and common sense are inversely correlated. It's no wonder Castro hoped Bush wouldn't be "as stupid as he seems." For forty years the dictator has been surrounded and visited by brilliant people who swear that he's brilliant and benevolent—and if Bush were indeed a dimwit, he might see right through Castro and conclude that all those people willing to brave sharks, drowning, dehydration, and firing squads to escape from Cuba actually recognize something that the dictator's brilliant admirers do not.

Of course, the same people who question the president's intelligence also tend to believe that he's a first-class liar who's been lying about, among many things, the reasons we went to war in Iraq. But that's where they saw off their own limbs, for surely this cranially challenged president can't be both a dunce and the architect of an elaborate house built on lies.

No, decades from now, when the history of this conflict can be judged by facts and not emotion, I'm reasonably certain that the president's actions will be seen with the same favor enjoyed now by Churchill, even though the former prime minister led a far-from-perfect war. And then volumes will be written about the wisdom of this president's course of action, mistakes included.

It gives me pleasure to think that, somewhere, Mr. Sloane will be reading those books and sharing their stories with young people who come by to say hello. One of them, no doubt, will be the story of what a newspaper editorial writer said about the president: "The cheek of every American must tingle with shame as he reads the silly, flat, and dishwatery utterances of the man who has to be pointed out to intelligent foreigners as the President of the United States."

The newspaper was the *Chicago Times*, the year was 1863, the president was Abraham Lincoln, and the speech he'd just given filled with such "dishwatery utterances" was the Gettysburg Address.

THE SOUND OF SILENCE

★   ★   ★

If you look closely at me on my TV show, you'll see that in a number of the factories we visit I have foam plugs tucked into my ears. That's not because I'm overly sensitive to noise, but because OSHA demands that everyone exposed to a prevailing decibel level considered too high must wear them to prevent hearing loss.

Funny that the government gets involved in workplaces where workers with common sense—and common courtesy—would undoubtedly take care of their hearing without edict. How do I know that? I talk to these people. I ask questions. I eat lunch with them and maybe dinner, too. I know what they think, who they are, and what they're made of. And believe me, no one has to tell the guy running a punch press at Cutco or the stamper at Pyrex that he better do something to protect his senses. Not only does he load in the ear plugs, as required, he then goes about eight steps better by covering them with expensive noise-canceling earphones—which he may have bought himself on his own dime—because foam plugs alone don't provide enough protection.

So here's what I wonder: If the government believes that ordinary people won't act in their own best interests without nanny bureaucrats threatening to whack their employer's hands like a German nun with a ruler, as it obviously does, then why don't some Big Brothers step in to keep me from going deaf when the idiot next to me at the stoplight has 50 Cent cranked up loud enough to get Osama bin Laden's home number out of terrorists at Gitmo—assuming the ACLU didn't consider that unconstitutionally cruel and unusual? How come that mutton-head's super-subatomic mega-shock woofer is allowed to rumble through my car and body like a lithotripsy machine? No question, this is the kind of situation where I'd really welcome the feds. I say we get those OSHA inspectors out on the street where they can do some good.

Fat chance, though.

And not just because the "O" in OSHA stands for "occupational," but because sometime over the last couple of decades a committee must've gotten together and decided to outlaw public silence and propriety. At some point, it seems, the idea of no sound, no noise, no music became quaint notions—like modesty, chastity, and shame.

Take ballparks, for example—the largest public place most of us visit. Used to be that you'd go to a ballgame and actually watch the game itself—nothing but you, the crack of the bat, the roar of the crowd, a few songs on the organ, the friend you were with, and the guy behind you blowing raspberries at the ump. That was both the beauty of baseball and the rhythm of baseball; you had time to reflect between pitches and anticipate the action, thinking along with the manager, or maybe just talking quietly to your friend.

No more. Now the stadiums program in music between

pitches—and the music programmer is that muttonhead with the superwoofer. Rock music, rap music, heavy metal—these aren't the rhythm of baseball. Not only do the songs sound like fingernails on a blackboard to at least half the crowd, but the driving beat doesn't jibe with the leisurely game, making it seem even slower than it already is. And talking? Forget about it. You can get hoarse from shouting to your seatmate over whatever OutKast seems to be singing about.

Apparently baseball got the idea of piping in hard music from basketball. Just as the basketball owners had to do something to cover up the fact that an elegant team game was being turned into five one-on-one match-ups by selfish players eager to pad their stats and therefore their contracts, the baseball owners must've figured that loud music would distract us from noticing how badly the quality of play has deteriorated since they began paying crotch-grabbing chaw spitters enough to buy small countries on guaranteed contracts, the guarantee referring to the fact that they'll rarely try hard enough to possibly hurt themselves until the last year of their deals.

No wonder the stadium has to flash messages on the electronic board telling us when to cheer. I hate that, darn it. I don't want anyone telling me when to cheer or "Make Noise!!!" I'll cheer when something happens worth cheering about, and as far as making noise is concerned—trust me, they don't have a clue what they're ordering up when they ask me. I'll give them noise, all right.

Now, if they ever command "Boo!" after some $10-million-a-year outfielder strikes out with runners on first and second in the bottom of the ninth and the score tied, when all he had to do was hit a lazy grounder to the right in order to get the runners over, but oh no, he had to swing from the heels at a pitch in the dirt—count me in, I'm all boos. Until then, forget the messages and turn off the music.

Of course, music is everywhere you go these days, not just in sports stadiums. Insidiously, it moved from elevators to the lobbies, and isn't just inside stores now but also outside, on walkways and sidewalks and outdoor patios. You can't escape it, even if all you want to do is sit at a little plastic table outside the Baskin-Robbins and eat your chocolate chip. There, up above you, pumping out of tinny speakers is likely to be the long version of "House of the Rising Sun."

Honestly, I like music. No, I *love* music—but I want to hear it when I want to hear it, and if I want to hear it in public I'll carry my iPod, not a fat boombox, so I don't intrude on anyone else.

Same with TV. Television belongs at home or in sports bars—where you can turn it on and off or change the channel or leave, depending—not in public. It irritates me to walk through airports and have to hear CNN blaring from monitors located with mathematical precision, so that unless you're deaf (or armed with earplugs) you're never out of earshot. All I can think of is that it's too bad cell sites aren't placed as strategically as airport TVs. If they were, we'd never drop another cell call.

No wonder people are on edge and rude in the big cities, where the bombardment is constant and silence is considered a disease. Whether or not they're consciously aware of it, they sure sense that there's no sanctuary, no respite, no relief.

All that music and all those talking heads, maybe people just become inured to the pervasive cacophony—or they're conditioned to try and accommodate it.

When I'm emperor, silence will be the cure.

Until then, I've decided to fight a series of guerilla battles, starting with drivers who have PA systems in their cars. Courtesy of Jerry Gibson, the man behind Gibson Bagpipes in Willoughby, Ohio, I insert my CD of the New York Fire Department Emerald Society Pipes and Drums and crank it up as loud as I can, then slowly roll down my window. Bagpipe music, you see, magically cuts through rap music, no matter how loud it is. The bagpipes go screaming into the muttonhead's car like flying snakes. He can't help but hear them—and turn down Ludacris, to make sure he hears what he thinks he's hearing. And when he's sure, he turns toward me. And I smile.

In the duel between bagpipes and rap, music wins every time. I just hope I'm long gone by the time nostalgia rap starts coming out of elevators.

WHERE NOBODY KNOWS YOUR NAME

★   ★   ★

Ever since playing Cliff on *Cheers,* I tend to avoid bars. It's not that I mind so much when someone asks where Norm is, or why don't I have my mailman uniform on, or am I familiar with some little-known fact about creosote—though I could happily survive without hearing any of those quips again. No, I like staying out of bars—especially, particularly, deliberately in the Boston area—because, one, I don't drink beer, which is generally what well-meaning patrons send over without asking, meaning that I either have to drink it or seem rude; and two, being recognized as a Hollywood barfly is a lot like being a professional athlete out on the town: some jerk-off usually wants a piece of you, to prove you're not better than he is. There may be other reasons, too, that I keep off barstools, but I don't have to remember them as long as I adhere to the first two.

And yet, there I was at a Boston bar with the owner of an area factory, a few hours after we finished filming in his place. We'd not only hit it off personally, but his whole crew had been incredibly welcoming, so I couldn't very well say no thanks when he asked. Nor did I want to.

To my surprise and pleasure, I didn't hear a single "Cliff" or "Norm," or any questions. I was just another guy at the bar having drinks with a buddy. Either they didn't recognize me under my baseball cap, or they didn't want to disturb me. But the place was packed, and it was fun—exactly why folks like Cliff and his friends would spend their nights at a place like Cheers.

Richard, the factory owner, was on my left. We talked about how many hoops you have to jump through these days to stay in business, and how a lot of people in America have come to see business as the enemy of prosperity, not its creator.

To my right was an attractive young woman talking to a man on the next stool. Every time I glanced over, I saw them playing yes-no.

Then, in walked somebody wearing a leather jacket, a T-shirt, blue jeans, boots, chains, neck tattoos, and piercings from the nose, eyebrow, ears, and chin. This was one mean and ugly dude—only, in the immortal words of Steve Tyler, the dude was a lady. A pissed-off lady, at that.

Evidently the woman next to me had once been the object of her affections, and now she was talking to a—gasp—man.

Men suck, declared the lady dude. Men are useless. They're jackasses, animals, scumbags, cretins—on and on she went for fifteen minutes (in X-rated language), attracting as much attention as she could, and going unchallenged.

"It's a diesel dyke," Richard whispered.

I hadn't been sure what a diesel dyke was—"Oh, so *that's* what you call her," I said—but I did know that in real life, you never worry about the loudmouth bully who walks into bars or wherever with a look-at-me-I'm-bad swagger and strut. If you're a man, strutting means you've got nothing to back it up. And if you've got the goods, you don't need to strut in a way that says "look at me." Every man understands that really tough guys are quiet—which was why, I'm guessing, everybody let her be. Watching her was a form of entertainment, not unlike a car wreck.

Still, I found her annoying and distracting. And when a few people walked out I concluded that they'd been driven away by the racket. If the bartender had been a man, no doubt he would've told her to shut her trap. But behind the bar was a tiny redheaded beauty with green eyes and white teeth—who looked at me in a way that said "Help!" I decided I couldn't wait anymore for someone else to play cop.

"Hey," I said, "miss"—which got her attention and ticked her off good. "Excuse me."

She glared and began swaggering like John Wayne. The bar got quiet, just like in a John Wayne movie.

I said, "You may not know this, but you're acting like the kind of man that even men think are jackasses. It's not a good thing."

Apparently she was the kind of person who didn't take well to psychological insights, because now she came right at me and took a swing at my face. Which I thought was kind of stupid.

I grabbed her arm and held her for a moment against the bar. "This," I said, "is exactly what I'm talking about."

Now she was spitting and hissing.

"Maybe it's better if you go home," I said, letting her up. "And behave yourself."

As she left, the place erupted in—dare I say it—cheers. Not

only was there a round on the house, but most everybody else insisted on buying me a drink, too.

And the next morning, wondering as I awakened when and how I'd gotten back to my hotel room, I painfully remembered the other reason I tend to avoid bars.

MONDAY MORNING POLITICS

★ ★ ★

I try to stay away from arguing about politics, religion, and dog pedigrees. It's a losing battle, even when you win. But sometimes you just can't help yourself.

The fight, such as it was, actually had its roots in my show's visit to factories in the South. We were there at the height of the "Bush lied, millions died" hysteria, when you couldn't turn on the news or open a paper without another top Democrat claiming betrayal and pretending that he or she hadn't voted for the war's authorization. That seemed to bring out the cynical common sense in a lot of the locals I met, especially throughout Arkansas, where President Bush's predecessor hailed from politically and in every other way.

Some Arkansans, I got the sense, feel responsible—okay, guilty—for having given the country Bill Clinton. Several people I spoke to blamed him for "starting this war" by not reacting to the first World Trade Center terrorist bombing a month after his inauguration, and then doing more or less nothing when terrorists blew up two American embassies in Africa, the Khobar Towers barracks in Saudi Arabia, and the USS *Cole* in Yemen's waters, killing in all more than a hundred and wounding thousands. When Sudan offered to turn over Osama bin Laden to the United States, the Clinton administration refused to accept him on the grounds that terrorism was a law-enforcement issue and any indictment might not stick for lack of "evidence." And yet Clinton had described Saddam Hussein as a clear and present danger to not only America but also to the free world when, in 1998, he introduced and signed the "Iraq Liberation Act" that called for regime change.

But actually taking concrete steps to effect that change—well, that wasn't in Clinton's makeup or plan. Which was why, in Arkansas, I also heard people liken Clinton to Neville Chamberlain, the British prime minister who appeased Hitler up to and including Germany's taking of Czechoslovakia. Ever since then, Chamberlain's name has been synonymous with appeasement, and some people I met in Arkansas said that they hope future history books refer to Clinton with the same disdain.

I gently pointed out that if you travel that road, you have to first blame Jimmy Carter, who let the secular shah of Iran fall in favor of the first modern Islamic theocracy, which governs according to the strictest and most restrictive rules of the Koran. Then you must include Ronald Reagan, who emboldened the Islamic fanatics by withdrawing our Marines from their peace-keeping mission in Lebanon after a suicide bomber killed 241 people. Finally, you have to hold the first President Bush accountable for leaving Saddam Hussein in power after the 1991 Gulf War.

"But at least," I said, "we can agree that our current president is no appeaser."

"Sure he is," one man insisted.

"How? Who does he appease?"

"The left. The press. The Democrats. All they do is rag on him—how he's a liar and all. All these freakin' Monday morning quarterbacks . . ."

My new buddy had a point, so there was no argument there. For two years the president had been appeasing those who kept shouting—and shouting ever louder—about why we went to war in Iraq. As soon as it was clear that we would not be finding huge stockpiles of weapons of mass destruction, the critics began piping up about how "Bush lied." As though finding WMDs had been the *only* stated reason for the war, or that it hadn't been the chief worry of his predecessor's administration.

Even so, I tended to agree with President Bush's decision to say nothing. The claims were too ridiculous to merit any kind of response without seeming beneath the office. That lesson was taught by President Clinton's almost daily response to his political adversaries, which had sometimes sounded petty and almost embarrassing.

And then, for me, came the golden moment of unhingement—and it came almost the day I returned home to California from the South: Clinton gave a speech calling the Iraq war a "big mistake."

The words by themselves were bad enough, but as it turned out, he'd uttered them to Arab students.

In Dubai.

My blood heated.

It wasn't so much the infuriating idea that a former president would criticize the foreign policies of a sitting president— a phenomenon rare, if not unheard of, before Jimmy Carter began doing it a couple of years ago. And it wasn't even that

Clinton, like Hollywood celebrities in search of adoration, did it on foreign soil, where he knew he'd receive a rousing ovation.

No, it was my realization that President Bush's failure to respond to the thousand little lies told about him had allowed the Big Lie chorus to drown out the rest of the country—so much so that polls showed nearly half the populace believing that the president of the United States was a liar. No doubt that was why his purely political predecessor, angling for a return to the White House through his wife, believed that he could shamelessly disavow his own previous beliefs, statements, and actions, and criticize his successor.

Clinton's speech, it appeared, was a wake-up call for the Bush administration. The president and some of his cabinet immediately went on the offensive, pointing out that his critics in Congress saw the same data he saw and yet voted to grant him their blessings to send out the troops.

The facts were on the president's side, and anyone who actually cared about the truth, instead of taking whatever pleasure might be found in repeating the lie that the president was a liar, could have referred to several of America's most prominent columnists. Many of them skillfully detailed the cynicism and credulousness one would have to suffer from in order to believe the Big Lies. Some even mentioned the comprehensive Duelfer Report, written in late 2004 by a CIA agent working with the Iraq Survey Group. At the time of the report's release, the mainstream press and the president's critics jumped all over its declaration that there were no weapons of mass destruction to be found in Iraq.

But in fact the report also stated—with only a rare, brief, and dismissive mention in the mainstream press and no mentions by political critics—that Saddam Hussein had been assured by the French and Russians, both of whom were gorging themselves on the UN's oil-for-food trough, that America would not fight without UN approval; and that they, the French and Russians, would get the sanctions against Iraq lifted. Leave aside the unavoidable implication that war might have been averted if not for our venal "allies" and focus on the unavoidable probability that the sanctions would have been lifted if not for the war. Then what? At that point, said the report, Saddam would've quickly reconstituted his WMD program—perhaps within a few weeks. So the facts were hiding in plain sight for anyone willing to see them.

But of course, if you're not looking for the facts or you choose to ignore them, you could take refuge in Clinton's wake and use his Dubai pronouncement as an "Aha, gotcha" piece of so-called evidence in support of your opinion—as a film producer friend of mine did. "See?" he said. "Clinton tells it like it is."

Maybe it was that I'd just come back from Arkansas, where I'd been surrounded by people with common sense, which isn't quite so common in the zip codes near where I live. Or maybe I'd just reached the breaking point with the "Bush lied, people died" school of bumper-sticker thought. Whatever it was, I broke my self-imposed prohibition against one-on-one political arguments.

"Do you really believe what you're saying?" I half asked and half accused. "Do you really think there's no difference between being wrong about something and lying about it?"

"Bush manipulated the data," he insisted.

"Really? I thought you guys thought he was so stupid, he couldn't do anything right. So which is it? Is he a fool or an evil genius?"

"We didn't have to go to war."

"Didn't anything change for you after September eleventh?" I asked.

"Yeah, back then, we had the sympathy of the world on our side. Bush squandered it."

"I'm curious . . . did we have the sympathy of the world on September tenth?"

"Right before the attacks? No, we didn't."

"Why not?"

"Because Bush was president."

"So the only way we can have the world's sympathy is if we're attacked and thousands die and we don't do anything about it."

"Well, Bush could've brought the world together after 9/11, but instead he made everybody hate us."

"Wasn't that Clinton's strategy—doing nothing after we were attacked?"

"The world loved us when Clinton was president."

"Right," I said. "Bin Laden loved us so much when Clinton was president that he declared war against America and began plotting our demise."

"But it happened on Bush's watch."

"So what, exactly, should he have done after 9/11?" I asked.

I have to say that I've weighed all sides of the war in Iraq, and, whether or not we ultimately succeed there, I don't think its righteousness can be seriously questioned—unless, of course, you buy into the war-for-oil argument, which is easily countered with an unanswerable question: If all we wanted was oil, why didn't we just lift the sanctions and go in there and buy what we wanted, instead of spending hundreds of billions of dollars and leaving all the oil for the Iraqis?

Oh, and then there's the "we're fighting for Halliburton" argument, which is just as easily countered with the fact that Halliburton has done less well financially *since* the war than it did *before* the war.

Which leaves us with the "support our troops, bring them home" argument. That one is answered with the fact that, unlike Vietnam, in this war our troops overwhelmingly support what we're doing, because they can see the progress every day—even if the American people, who rely primarily on mainstream media reports for their news, are kept in the dark. And, yes, while three or four or five thousand dead American soldiers is a terrible price to pay, it's also an historical anomaly in warfare—an astonishingly low number for what's been accomplished, including several free elections, the restoration of a complete economy, and the birth of a free press. I wonder if the same people who decry this war because of the "cost" in lives would've said the same about our Civil War, fought to eliminate slavery and keep the union together. In that war, six hundred thousand soldiers died—a full 2 percent of America's population. Two percent in today's terms equals 6 million dead. Yes, that war was fought on this soil, and Iraq is thousands of miles away. But with the technologies of the twenty-first century, every country is right next door.

And every country we fight and defeat is immediately the beneficiary of our generosity. We are the only country in recorded history that uses its own money to make its former foes whole without imposing American viceroys.

It's true that mistakes have probably been made in how we waged the war. But mistakes are made in *every* war, just as they're made in every large-scale human operation. World

War II, for example, was fraught with both tactical errors and political miscalculations that ended up costing countless American lives.

No, someday—and not a moment too soon—historians will remember for us what the tenor of the times was before we went to war in Iraq. And that story will begin with the declaration from the mouth of Representative Cynthia McKinney while the ashes of the World Trade Center were still smoldering. "We know," she said, "there were numerous warnings of the events to come on September eleventh. What did this administration know and when did it know it, about the events of September eleventh?"

Farfetched as the claim may have seemed—the utterance of a leftist conspiracy lunatic—the Georgia congresswoman was the first but would not be the last to accuse President Bush of having purposefully ignored intelligence that predicted the imminent use of hijacked planes as missiles.

Soon the world heard an echo from Senator Hillary Clinton—on the Senate floor, no less: "What did Bush know and when did he know it?" she asked.

As did Howard Dean. The then-presidential candidate passed along the "theory"—as he called it—on radio that Bush was "warned ahead of time by the Saudis." Later came the pronouncements of former Nixon aide John Dean, he of "a cancer on the presidency" fame. Promoting a book about the Bush administration titled *Worse than Watergate*, the convicted felon wrote that the president "likely" ignored "the potential of terrorists [flying] airplanes into skyscrapers."

By then a headline in the *New York Times* had declared, "Bush Was Warned bin Laden Wanted to Hijack Planes," which the *Washington Post* confirmed with its "Bush Was Told of Hijacking Dangers." These stories, among hundreds, referred to comments by the co-chair of the independent and bipartisan 9/11 Commission, Thomas Kean, synopsizing the first findings that suggested that the attacks could have been prevented.

The clamor inevitably reached the morning TV chatfests (Katie Couric: "What did Bush know and when did he know it?") and the rest of the media, growing so pervasive that it sounded like hillside coyotes celebrating a kill. Its high point would later appear in the person of Richard Clarke, former National Security Council chief of counterterrorism. His best-selling book *Against All Enemies: Inside America's War on Terror* received an ungodly amount of attention for his claims that the president and his team had remained willfully ignorant of the threat posed by al-Qaeda.

Remember all this? Sure you do.

What you may not remember was that the source of all this hysteria was a single presidential daily briefing, given to the president on August 6, 2001. The report said nothing about hijacked planes being flown into buildings and indeed admitted that "some of the more sensational threat reporting" could not be corroborated. It did, however, refer to bin Laden's stated goals of bringing the fighting to America—claims bin Laden himself had made on ABC television three years before—as well as the luckily foiled millennium bomber of 1999 (when only a sharp-eyed border guard, who noticed sweat on the would-be bomber's brow, kept Los Angeles International Airport from being blown up) and the African embassy bombings a year earlier.

Given the amount of willful amnesia going around, it seems

necessary to mention that these events happened under the previous president's watch, and that the millennium bombing plot in particular was played down immediately afterward by then–national security adviser Sandy Berger, who assured the country that it was not part of a more concerted effort to attack our homeland. Yet an after-action report—possibly the one he later stuffed down his sock while "preparing" for his testimony in front of the 9/11 Commission—suggested that this had likely been confirmation of al-Qaeda's operational presence on the ground in the United States.

For their part, the mainstream media happily reported Berger's and Clinton's assurances that the terrorists weren't among us, but then ignored the after-action statement. And a year later, in early 2004, when the 9/11 Commission issued a 150-page report stating that terrorists were already preparing to strike American soil, the media either ignored or gave short shrift to its findings: "States, terrorists, and other disaffected groups will acquire weapons of mass destruction, and some will use them. Americans will likely die on American soil, possibly in large numbers." The *New York Times* reported not a word, and even turned down an op-ed written by the commission chairs, former senators Gary Hart and Warren Rudman. So much for ignoring intelligence.

Now comes early 2003. Saddam Hussein has just failed to comply with his seventeenth United Nations resolution by—as even that useful-idiot, see-no-evil weapons inspector Hans Blix agreed—not providing a complete and detailed list of all WMD and ballistic missile capabilities. (What people tend also to forget is that it was up to Hussein to come clean, not up to us to seek and find the weapons if we could.) The resolution (1441) threatened "serious consequences" for failure to comply, but our so-called allies on the UN Security Council, France and Russia, apparently considered "serious consequences" to mean an eighteenth resolution—to be followed, I assume, by a nineteenth and more. Whispering in Hussein's ear that they wouldn't go along with any military action, they were promising to get the twelve-year-old sanctions against Iraq lifted, which in fact reflected a growing world opinion.

Back in Washington, the president and Congress had access to bales full of intelligence from around the world stating that Hussein had an active WMD program, including biological, chemical, and probably nuclear capabilities. Even the Egyptians were warning the president that Iraq was well-armed and dangerous. The Senate, having viewed that intelligence and consulted with international leaders, went on the record, both verbally and with a vote, supporting the notion that Saddam Hussein needed to go before he attacked America.

So then what?

Well, even if you buy the Democrats' claim that the president "misled a nation into war by cherry-picking intelligence," as John Kerry once droned, you're inconveniently stuck with the fact that a vast preponderance of that intelligence, rightly or wrongly, pointed unambiguously toward Iraq's status as a rogue state.

Now, you have to think about this from the president's point of view, as future historians will. Much of the country is calling for your head over your alleged failure to prevent 9/11 when *no* firm intelligence predicted such a thing. Do you really have any choice but to act on the overwhelming amount of *clear* evidence that says bad things are happening beneath hidden bunkers in Iraq? The answer, for anyone not blinded by hate, is no: you have no other way out than to fight preemptively. If you don't, well, heaven forbid another attack is made on American soil—with grotesque weapons, sold to al-Qaeda for a hefty fee, that came out of Iraq after sanctions were lifted and Saddam's WMD program was reconstituted.

At his impeachment trial, shortly before conviction, the shamed president would've been made to endure a verbatim recitation of the many dire warnings about Iraq and Saddam Hussein uttered by Democrats Ted Kennedy, Nancy Pelosi, Al Gore, Bill Clinton, Sandy Berger, and Madeleine Albright— none of whom would've been shy to note how many times they'd been on the record decrying Saddam's Iraq and urging immediate action.

"Iraq is a long way from [here]," Secretary of State Albright said on February 18, 1998, "but what happens there matters a great deal here. For the risks that the leaders of a rogue state will use nuclear, chemical, or biological weapons against us or our allies is the greatest security threat we face."

She was right—which was why the president was right too, for acting as he did.

"So what, exactly, should he have done after 9/11?" I asked my producer friend.

"Brought the world together," he said.

"How?"

"It doesn't matter, because he wanted to go to war all along, even before 9/11. That was his plan."

"You're saying he knew about 9/11?"

"It wouldn't surprise me a bit. Maybe. Yeah, yeah, I believe that."

"Which means the president of the United States ignored

warnings that potentially tens of thousands of Americans would die in an attack."

"Right."

And with that I went back to my self-imposed moratorium on political arguments. Expecting the facts to make a difference with some people is like trying to teach a pig to sing. As Mark Twain said, it wastes your time and really annoys the pig.

A RAT IS A PIG
IS A DOG IS A BOY

★   ★   ★

For reasons that will soon be obvious, I prefer not to name the company involved in pharma-technologies that I visited some time ago. I asked one of the executives whether they sometimes used animals in testing.

"Well," he said, scrunching his face as though trying to keep down a bad tamale, "I'd rather not say."

And who could blame him for that? These days the country is mad with self-righteous "activists" who break into science labs, smash equipment, and "rescue" testing animals because they believe, for instance, "There is no rational basis for saying that a human being has special rights. A rat is a pig is a dog is a boy. They're all mammals." Or that, "Six million Jews died in concentration camps, but six billion broiler chickens will die this year in slaughterhouses."

While both of those jaw-dropping statements came from the mouth of Ingrid Newkirk, founder of People for the Ethical Treatment of Animals (PETA) neither sentiment is unique to her (nor do they exhaust her jaw-dropping arsenal). Across the country countless individuals and groups (including the Humane Society of America) believe that humans and animals are of equal value on that great cosmic scale of importance. To them, your daughter is worth the same as that mouse in your attic—and so occasionally they bust into labs in order to "liberate" mice on whom experiments are being conducted that might save your daughter's life someday. Just two examples: At the University of Arizona, members of the Animal Liberation Front broke into a lab, stole a thousand rodents, and destroyed two years' worth of research on treatments and vaccines for a bacteria that causes fatal diarrhea in *human beings*. And a group that calls itself PAWS was responsible for shutting down a University of Washington study into how mothers transmit SIV (the simian form of HIV) to their infants.

That Animal Liberation Front and PAWS and other "animal rights" groups are apparently more violent than PETA only works to legitimize PETA: their violence and wanton destruction make PETA's lunacy seem, by contrast, somehow sane and therefore deserving of attention. What makes PETA stand apart from other activist groups is Newkirk's charisma and rhetorical brilliance, which also attract creative marketing tacticians to continually devise mind-boggling "campaigns" that grab the media spotlight and thereby attract notice.

I'm not sure Hollywood celebrities are more vulnerable to PETA's lure than most people, or whether their fame makes it seem so. Bill Maher, Alicia Silverstone, Rene Russo, and Kim Basinger are just a few of the screen famous who lend their names and stature to this group.

It was Woody Harrelson, I think, who invited some PETA staff to our *Cheers* offices at Paramount Studios several years ago. I remember sitting at my desk when there was a knock at the door. Three or four of them walked in, well-dressed, smiling, politely spoken, bearing gifts of brochures and pamphlets about animal "abuses" somewhere.

One of them asked me if I was an animal lover.

"Oh, of course," I said, telling them about some of the wonderful dogs I'd owned, including the half-wolf, half-husky I had while living more or less in the wilds of Vermont. He'd been quilled by a porcupine and was suffering, so I had to lay him down on his back and yank the quills from his snout one by one. "After that," I said, "our relationship kind of soured."

They blanched at the story, but then so did I, reliving it. Then I told them about some of the dogs I'd paid to have buried in an animal cemetery, complete with headstones; and a dog I'd rushed two hours down the San Diego freeway, to put him on dialysis; and the weeklong horseback ride I'd taken in the backcountry of Wyoming, looking for grizzly bears to shoot—with a camera.

Well, they must've sensed that I was one of them, a kindred spirit—and, best of all, another valuable celebrity eager to spread the issue du jour. They began pressing their point about my signing on for personal appearances and photographs and whatever else they could think of, including cash, in support of the good fight.

"Wait a second," I said. "Are you the folks who promote destroying labs of scientists looking for cures?"

"Yeah, we support that," the second guy said. "We support destroying medical labs that work with animals."

By the look of triumph on his face, he must've believed that was what I wanted to hear.

"Let me tell you something," I said. "If my kid had a disease, and if scientists convinced me I could cure his disease by biting off the heads of puppies in Times Square, I'd say, 'Hand me a schnauzer.'"

And with that there came a collective sharp intake of breath—three sets of lungs simultaneously—and some staggering backwards, then holding onto the curtains for balance. Within moments, they stomped out of there.

In their leather shoes.

There's something so Berlin 1932 about the whole animal rights and, for that matter, radical environmental movements. They're the preoccupations of a people with nothing important to worry about. The sheer decadence of the hundreds of thousands—if not millions—of people who swallow these messages suggests that we've somehow been too successful.

Only in a culture in which leisure time is as abundant as seawater could a movement like this exist. During times of serious existential threat—World War II, for example—the relative worth of lab rats wouldn't amount to even a blip on society's radar screen. Just as idle hands become the devil's playground, as the aphorism goes, affluence breeds lunacy and foolishness, which lead to moral confusion. If you don't think so, then try out the morality of PETA's handouts, given directly to kids, called "Your Daddy Kills Animals" and "Buckets of Blood."

The first is a comic book showing a wild-eyed, grinning madman gutting a fish and telling kids to keep their beloved puppies and kitties away from Dad because "he's hooked on killing." The second giveaway is an ersatz KFC take-home bucket filled with a bag of fake blood and fake bones, a bloodied plastic chicken, and a caricature of Colonel Sanders pulling a butcher's knife on a cowering chicken.

And then there's the flyer PETA passes out to children wherever they congregate during the holiday season—say, performances of *The Nutcracker.* It's a comic-book drawing of a woman plunging a knife into the belly of a trembling rabbit, as its own blood drips. The flyer tells kids to "ask your mommy how many dead animals she killed to make her fur clothes," and points out that "the sooner she stops wearing fur, the sooner the animals will be safe. Until then, keep your doggie or kitty friends away from mommy—she's an animal killer."

Yes, the First Amendment guarantees us the right to free speech, but free speech always has a cost. And in this case, the cost is to the fabric of society. Children being taught to think of their parents as murderers for putting food on the table can lead nowhere that anyone with common sense or historical sense should want to go. Remember the Hitler Youth in Nazi Germany? How kids were encouraged to rat out their parents for not being devoted enough to der Führer's Fatherland? That's what comes to my mind when I see PETA turning children against their parents. It's vile, disgusting, nauseating, and beyond the pale—or at least what *used to be* beyond the pale. A group like PETA that targets children's relationships to their parents should be ridiculed and shamed out of existence, not taken seriously and debated earnestly by people in the media and academia.

But that's exactly what happens every time PETA comes up with a newer, more outrageous campaign—just as slasher movies like *Halloween* had to devise ever-more-gruesome murders. Unlike slasher movies, though, PETA never goes away.

And why should it, when some of the most prominent people in the world bless it with money and esteem? People like Paul McCartney. The former Beatle told the BBC that he "wouldn't even dream of going" to China to perform his music, "in the same way I wouldn't go to a country that supported apartheid." Why? Because of the millions who were persecuted and executed during the Cultural Revolution (while the Beatles were at the peak of their popularity)? Or because of the brutal crackdown on democracy lovers in Tiananmen Square? Or maybe because China strictly enforces a one-child-per-couple policy, forcing unwanted abortions and leading millions to callously dump infant girls in shallow graves so that they can try again for a boy? Oh, maybe Sir Paul's refusal to perform is a protest in support of the political dissidents who are jailed and often tortured for daring to criticize the Chinese leadership on human rights.

Well, no, I'm sorry to say it's none of those. The reason Paul McCartney will never step foot professionally on the other side of the Great Wall is because—here it comes—of animal cruelty. Specifically, the fur trade.

"If they want to consider themselves a civilized nation," he declared, "they're going to have to stop this."

Think about that for a second. In McCartney's moral calculus, a nation's status as civilized or uncivilized is dependent on how it treats its animals, not its humans. That's a remarkable notion, one that sends a chill down my back. Even if you cut him some slack on ignorance—that is, not knowing better that China has one of the worst human-rights policies on earth— you then have to ask why a man who has literally everything is so ignorant of the truth.

The answer, I'm afraid, is why that pharmaceutical executive was reticent to answer my question about whether he ever used animals in testing.

"It's okay," I soothed him. "You're among friends."

"I don't know," he said, still reluctant—and possibly think-ing I had a hidden microphone with a direct connection to In-grid Newkirk.

"Let me guess," I said. "You only use animals when you have to—when there aren't any other ways to determine whether a drug really works and is safe."

"You know a lot about this?" he asked.

"I know that it's too bad the drug companies didn't test thalidomide on animals in the forties and fifties before giving it to the mothers of all those poor people who were born without limbs or worse. I know that every single AIDS drug has been animal tested. I know that a really promising drug for people with spinal cord injuries couldn't have gotten this far without some cats giving their all. And I know that human beings are more valuable than animals."

"I agree," he said, and that was all the answer I needed.

Pass the schnauzer.

ALIENS AMONG US

★   ★   ★

For my TV show, we visit forty factories a season, and nowhere have I seen what most of us would call an "easy" job. True, not all of them need a strong back or stronger antiperspirant, but every one of them requires at least a certain toughness.

Yet I keep reading in the press how Americans supposedly won't do certain jobs, and that's why we have to let people sneak into the country to do them. And do them they will, since they're here illegally and can't get any other kind of job but these "crap" jobs Americans allegedly won't do.

The operative word here is "illegal"—both as an adjective and noun. It's illegal to come into the country without authorization, and it's illegal to hire illegals. But illegals keep coming because they keep getting jobs from legals, which means that we're all complicit in a national criminal enterprise.

To rationalize that, we've quietly agreed to agree that illegals are bailing us out—picking strawberries that would go unpicked if they weren't here and digging ditches for cable TV that wouldn't be laid if they weren't there with shovels. Then we wink and let more of them sneak in, even leaving water along the way to keep them from getting dehydrated in the hot Sonoran desert when they cross, so that by the time they hit the streets of America they're refreshed and ready to sweat at the jobs "Americans won't do." No less than the president of the United States buys into this, insisting that we really don't want illegals here and are doing everything we can to keep them out, but what can we do about it, given that there are tons of jobs Americans just won't do?

Here's what I want to know: Which Americans don't want these jobs? Please point to them.

When I was growing up, young people like me did those jobs, just as other young people had always done them. True, these weren't anybody's dream jobs, but we did them because we needed the money and those were the jobs that were available until you'd worked your way up the ladder or learned a skill that got you off the ladder. Every kid I knew in Bridgeport raked leaves, cut grass, washed windows, dug ditches, hammered nails, shoveled snow, cut lumber, hauled trash—whatever anyone was offering to pay for.

Trust me, nothing instilled discipline and focus faster than those "crap" jobs. If you didn't want to do them all your life, you had to do what it took to not have to. In fact, the hardest job I ever had led directly to my current career. I was working as a deckhand on an oyster boat, which is only a little harder than backpacking with bowling balls. One afternoon I met with an actor I'd known at college, who offered me the lead in a play booked for the Stowe Playhouse in Vermont. It was for no pay, he advised, but I'd get a place to live, in the basement of the playhouse, and board. "Whaddya say?" I looked at him, then at the boat, then at him, then at the boat, then said, "Let's go."

Americans won't work hard jobs? Since when? This country was built on a principle called the Protestant work ethic, which distinguished us from every other nation-state in the world. Didn't take but fifty or so years after the Constitution for Americans to have one of the world's highest standards of living, virtually no starvation, and literacy levels that put us to shame now. No wonder the Irish, then the Germans, then the Italians and Jews, followed by Asians, and then everyone else wanted to come here, including my family and yours. And yes, they're still lined up to come—and still pouring over the porous border in the dark of night.

I understand why. Everyone does. They come because this is still the land of opportunity, and compared to where they're from, it's utopia. If I lived in a dusty town in central Mexico and looked around at my parents and brothers and uncles and saw the same dismal prospects for my future, I'd sneak in here too—then work my tail off to make as much money as I could and send it home to them.

So I don't blame them. But how long can our country survive when unskilled illegal workers keep flooding the country, changing the dynamics of everything by the force of their numbers?

Put aside the damage to the overloaded county hospital systems and public schools, and the billions of untaxed dollars that leave the country, and focus on how this unending supply of illegals drives down wages not only for American citizens and legal aliens, but also for other illegals. You want to know one reason why Americans "don't want those jobs"? It's because the laws of supply and demand have made janitors and house painters and window washers and nail pounders and a hundred other occupations that used to pay a decent wage into perpetually entry-level jobs for which there's always a waiting list.

Where I live, the gardeners complain that their clients won't chip in an extra few bucks per house to pay for the steep rise in gasoline. And why don't the homeowners? Because they don't have to. If one gardener raises his rates, there are a dozen more behind him willing to take the job at an even lower wage. No wonder the cost of lawn mowing hasn't gone up here in seven years.

The irony is that many of the same activists who protest against American companies like Nike for "exploiting workers" in third-world countries are the loudest advocates of opening the borders. They apparently don't realize that in countries where Nike operates, people willingly take those jobs at an hourly rate that's low by our standards but livable by theirs, given how many others there are willing to do the job and how few jobs there are total. Meanwhile, the protestors seem not to notice that by encouraging illegal immigration, they're creating the same exploitative conditions in this country that they decry over there. What they're encouraging is a permanent servant class that they would decry in any other country.

The people here who can least afford it are those who are hurt the most by this uncontrolled flood of immigration. At present rates, America will soon look and behave like a third-world country, with the middle class nonexistent and society divided into Haves, who can offer jobs, and Have-Nots, who'll be forced to take them.

It's a house of cards we're building, one that rests on the flimsy notion that we *need* illegals. But do we? Do we really?

Just for the sake of argument, let's say yes; let's say that Americans really don't want those jobs anymore at any price. Now let's ask why. Why would that be? What's changed in the last twenty years?

Hmmm. Well, could be that we've sissified a generation of kids—both boys and girls. Nowadays parents send them out wearing football helmets and hazmat suits just to play in the neighborhood. But it's not really play; it's a "playdate"—supervised, structured, prearranged. Any possible danger or risk has been vacuumed out, along with any vestiges of spontaneity. Parents today, incited by fears of omnipresent perverts and murderers, actually discourage their children from going outside and living real lives.

I can't remember the last time I saw a posse of kids on their bikes, getting into some sort of mischief the way my buds and I used to. We'd hop on our Schwinns first thing in the morning, governed by only one parental edict: be back before the street lights come on—or else. Other than that, we were on our own, sometimes spending the day chasing sirens, even if the fire trucks or ambulances ended up ten miles away. Those were real childhood adventures that you can't get from video games, television, or parents' good intentions—and they taught us lessons that are still paying off today.

A few years ago, when we lived on Vashon Island near Seattle, a young man from Los Angeles came up to visit. For the first few days, he stumbled every time he crossed the field to the orchard. I asked if he was okay.

"Yeah," he said, "it's just that I've never walked on uneven ground before."

Later we got on my boat for an excursion on the sound. After I filled the tank, he noticed a few drops of liquid on the deck and asked what they were. Gasoline, I told him.

"Oh," he said, "I always thought gas was black."

Now, this kid isn't different from tens of millions of young men and women who've never had to walk on uneven ground, never seen gasoline, never earned the kind of wisdom and common sense that comes only from doing things and taking chances. So what kinds of jobs will he work at, and what is he qualified to do? I don't know. But I do understand that it's no wonder the people filling "crap" jobs in America are those who weren't raised in a hermetic bubble. Unlike a lot of Americans, it seems, they know the difference between a hard day's work and a load of crap.

FEAR ITSELF

★ ★ ★

A few years ago I was visiting factories in the Northeast with my crew when the bird flu story finally kicked into overdrive—the first of many times. It would be a pandemic, declared the newscasters and reporters. Millions dead. Maybe hundreds of millions. Worse than the 1918 flu epidemic. Whatever.

People I met were frightened. Terrified, actually. They told me so over water-cooler talk during breaks. Some factory managers admitted they were thinking of issuing surgical masks and gloves to their employees "because you can be contagious and not know it, and by the time you feel sick, in a place like this we could have a hundred people infected."

One factory owner told me he planned to stock up on Tamiflu, if he could get his hands on it, just in case.

"But the doctors aren't even sure Tamiflu will be effective against bird flu," I pointed out.

"Doesn't matter," he said. "It can't hurt. And psychologically, if nothing else, it's a boost."

I asked what precautions he'd taken against SARS, when that respiratory disease was knocking people down in the Far East and Toronto, and the press was wild with speculation and predictions of epidemics, even a pandemic.

"None, really," he said, "but we sure worried about it."

"Somehow," I said, "I don't think your worrying is what kept the disease away." Not surprisingly, he ignored that.

"It's very scary what's going on," he lamented.

"Yes, it is," I said, but I wasn't thinking of bird flu or SARS or any other epidemic.

I was thinking of the boogeyman that seems never to leave us: fear itself.

Like Lon Chaney, fear has a thousand disguises and faces. It seems there's always something to be afraid of. Knock down one—say, anthrax, which almost closed the country in late 2001—and another pops up; say, a chemical attack, which caused a run on plastic sheeting and duct tape a few months later.

I remember walking through Costco at the height of the chemical-attack fears and running into a woman—who, as it happens, is married to one of the biggest stars in television history—with a large cart literally filled to the brim with rolls of duct tape. Why? I asked her.

"To protect ourselves," she said, explaining that her husband would've come to do this himself but didn't want anyone recognizing him—as *everyone* would have—walking around with two hundred rolls of duct tape.

My instinct was to tell her that they were being silly, but it was none of my business, and anyway I could imagine her answer: *How do you know? How do you know we're not going to be attacked tomorrow?*

And the truth is, I don't know; not really. Bad things do happen, and they happen to good people every day—car crashes, plane crashes, cancer, diabetes. The list is endless. Literally.

But it's also true that people, good and bad, are more likely to believe that catastrophes are imminent than they are to believe that everything is going to be all right and that the worst that our imaginations can muster rarely comes true—which is far more often the case.

Maybe that's why bad news races all the way around the world before good news can cross the street. The moment you wake in the morning and switch on the television or radio or unfold the newspaper, you're bombarded with reports of the next big worry—something terrible, something tragic, something bound to go horribly wrong. Something inevitable.

Something, in other words, to make you sorry you got out of bed in the first place.

No doubt that's the way it's been since Thag first painted the news on his cave wall that mastodons were going extinct, and fretted that now they'd never have enough meat to go around. A predisposition to bad news seems to be embedded in our DNA. We believe instinctively that what can go wrong will go wrong, and that our generation will be the last one on earth, soon to be exterminated by a meteor or nuclear holocaust or toxic lollipops or cataclysmic events foretold by Nostradamus or Scripture, whichever is worse. And first.

I remember cartoons in the 1950s poking fun at doomsayers who paraded city sidewalks with sandwich boards warning of impending disaster—in those days, a Russian nuclear attack. "The end is nigh," they would drone.

Well, the end was no more nigher then than it was in December of 999, when some Russian monks climbed into coffins shortly before the world's scheduled termination at the stroke of midnight in the year 1000. (How do you say "oops" in Russian?) But guess what? A millennium later, fear still ruled the day. We were frightened that planes would fall from the sky, banks would lose their records and turn everyone into paupers, stock markets would crash, whole states and countries would go dark, and nuclear missiles would launch themselves, creating Armageddon—and those were just a few of the more level-headed predictions of what would happen at the stroke of midnight that turned December 31, 1999, to January 1, 2000.

Such predictions were proclaimed loudly and incessantly by "experts" with a lot of impressive acronyms listed after their names. The Y2K Bug, they called it, referring to a presumed glitch in most of the world's computers that, beginning in the 1970s, had been recording the year by only its last two digits in order to save what was then valuable code space. They therefore lacked the capability to write "2000" when the day came. The result? Haywire computers wreaking unintentional havoc on the world.

The panic had begun to build, though slowly at first, after the oversight was discovered in the late 1990s. Scholarly journals and then the mainstream press picked up the story, detailing scenarios right out of *The Terminator,* with machines running amok. Soon Y2K was topic number one. Ancient computer programmers who understood ancient computer languages were hustled out of retirement and paid millions to rewrite all the codes before midnight, January 1, 2000. But the consensus was that they'd never finish in time; the End of Days was at hand.

Books about how to deal with the coming collapse became bestsellers, "expert" talking heads ate up hundreds of hours on TV and radio talk shows, and survivalist groups reported record attendance at their seminars. Tens of thousands withdrew their money from banks, sold their houses, liquidated their portfolios, bought property out in the desert or mountains, and moved into trailers and cabins that were "off the grid." That was the only way, "experts" insisted, to survive the chaos and looting and martial law that were sure to follow that fateful stroke of midnight.

And when it came? Nothing. Nothing more than a few light bulbs out for a second or two in East Timor. Other than that, Y2K quickly became Why2K—the joke of the millennium.

(If you're interested, I'd love to unload about a hundred garden tools and thirty-eight cases of ammo.)

It must be part of the human condition to expect our own nighness. Maybe it's the sheer incredibleness of life that makes us do it, not being able to accept its gifts graciously. Religious fundamentalists predict the End of Days will occur in our lifetime (as they have for every generation since Christ), while secular fundamentalists predict environmental holocausts will destroy Mother Earth any day now (as they have for every generation since Rachel Carson).

We must be fatalists. No newspaper ever went broke printing only bad news, and tycoons build mega-empires on the money we pay them to tell us what we pretend we don't want to hear. My sense is that this is a kind of defense mechanism: the inundation of doom and gloom acts as a buffer zone intended to keep us from being crushed when the sky does fall— or at least from being surprised that those big chunks are coming straight for our heads.

And while the sky never really does fall, there's irony galore attached to the pieces that sometimes do.

In the last five years we've suffered the worst terrorist attack in American history and the worst natural disaster in American history. But September 11 was not only preventable (by our intelligence agencies, which failed to connect the dots even though we'd been tracking the lead hijacker, Mohammed Atta, for a year), it was also not, if you'll recall, as ultimately murderous as it first seemed—not by a long shot, thank God. Early predictions at the time the second tower fell were that up to 50,000 people had perished, instead of the 2,800 who did die, while initial estimates of the dead at the Pentagon, where tens of thousands work, were at least ten times higher than the actual number of 189. We mourn for all the dead, but we also give thanks that there were not many more of them.

As for Hurricane Katrina, the National Weather Service had known for days that it was going to be an all-time whopper. So even before the federal response had a chance to react, Louisiana state and New Orleans city officials had already done everything wrong, thus ensuring maximum human misery. Waiting until the day before the storm made landfall to declare a mandatory evacuation, the city's mayor virtually guaranteed that thousands would suffer needlessly. He neither commandeered the school district's hundreds of buses to evacuate those unable to evacuate themselves, nor did he take Amtrak up on its offer to carry another few thousand residents to safety.

But of course in the mainstream media's distorted worldview—the one that sees the world as the alley around the corner where bullies pick on the powerless and hapless—the devastation of Katrina wasn't nearly apocalyptic enough. That's why the reportage also focused on this monster hurricane as a portent of storms to come, courtesy of global warming.

But is global warming a legitimate threat or the latest fear du jour? Consider this report from an April 1975 issue of *Newsweek*: "There are ominous signs that the Earth's weather patterns have begun to change dramatically and that these changes may portend a drastic decline in food production—with serious political implications for just about every nation on Earth."

An early description of global warming? Quite the opposite, actually. "The Cooling World" read the headline over the story about the findings of scientists at the National Oceanic and Atmospheric Administration who'd discovered a significant increase in snow pack and a 1 percent decrease in sunshine reaching the ground between 1964 and 1972, thus signaling the beginning of our planet's reversion to "Ice Age" weather conditions—and hence, disaster.

"Climatologists," the story concluded, "are pessimistic that political leaders will take any positive action to compensate for the climatic change, or even to allay its effects. . . . Scientists see few signs that government leaders anywhere are even prepared to take the simple measures of stockpiling food. . . ."

Of course, just fifteen years later, scientists who worked at some of these same agencies discovered something more heinous to worry about. What's interesting is that the effects of global warming are predicted to be just as cataclysmic as the mini Ice Age we apparently suffered, if briefly, in the mid-1970s. The difference now is that global cooling "experts" point to both colder weather and warmer weather as "proof" of global warming, which strikes me as akin to insisting that promiscuity is evidence of chastity.

But to the true global-warming believers, it's a sin to miss an evangelical opportunity. I doubt I'll ever forget the venomous remarks of the noted "environmentalist" Robert F. Kennedy Jr. a day before Katrina hit New Orleans. When it appeared as though the destruction would be "only" along the Mississippi coast and not in New Orleans, Kennedy gleefully poked a literary finger in the eye of Mississippi governor Haley Barbour—a former Republican bigwig—with an angry screed claiming that Katrina's devastation was karmic payback for Barbour's role in getting the Bush administration to decline to tax carbon dioxide as a pollutant.

"Well," wrote Kennedy, "the science is clear. This month, a study published in the journal *Nature* . . . linked the increasing prevalence of destructive hurricanes to human-induced global warming. Now we are all learning what it's like to reap the whirlwind of fossil fuel dependence which Barbour and his cronies have encouraged. Our destructive addiction has given us a catastrophic war in the Middle East and—now—Katrina is giving our nation a glimpse of the climate chaos we are bequeathing our children."

Meanwhile, Barbra Streisand told Diane Sawyer on *Primetime Live* (or was it *Saturday Night Live?*) that Katrina proved "that we are in a global warming emergency state, and that these storms are going to become more frequent, more intense."

Uh, not exactly. As it happens, the "busiest hurricane season on record," of which Katrina was the most notable event, seems to be part of Mother Nature's grand inscrutable plan. According to records kept by the National Hurricane Center and the National Climatic Data Center, among other agencies, hurricanes over the last 125 years—dating back to well before anyone ever used the term "fossil fuels"—have kept to cycles lasting twenty to thirty years. In fact, the 1900 Galveston hurricane that killed eight thousand, making it the deadliest storm on record, took place in the first year of a thirty-year period of relative calm, which was then followed by thirty years of above-average activity, including America's first recorded Category 5 storm in 1935. And that cycle was followed in turn by twenty-five years of below-average activity.

You might be interested to know that the storms of the 1960s were frequently blamed on nuclear testing, while 1969's monster hurricane, Camille, which killed hundreds and cost billions (striking roughly the same area as Katrina), was generally blamed on our Apollo 11 moon landing of a few months before. As for the period of wild hurricane activity we're in today, it appears to have begun in 1995, when, if memory serves, President Clinton was in office and Haley Barbour had zero power at the federal level.

The question is not whether the earth is warming up; it very likely is. The question is whether man-made activity bears responsibility for the warming, and also whether that warming is good, bad, or indifferent. And on those matters, there's hardly scientific consensus, no matter what you might read or hear (from the usual Chicken Littles). One doesn't have to be a climatologist or even know at what temperature water boils in order to understand that long before the first fossil-fueled machine—when, in fact, those fossils were just a gleam in some dinosaur's eye—earth's long history had already been marked by distinct periods of warm and warmer, cold and colder.

Nonetheless, the urge to blame something or somebody (particularly political foes), coupled nicely with fear (especially the fear of fear), has turned global warming into the trendiest of trendy doomsday scenarios. No less than the man who was five hundred Florida votes away from being president, Al Gore, calls global warming a more dangerous threat to our existence than terrorism—which creates a kind of compelling and persuasive argument for staying in bed with the covers pulled over your head.

Our ancient ancestors didn't have that option, so they took affirmative action by sacrificing virgins and babies to the fire. In that way, they saved themselves from storms, earthquakes, and giant apes. And if one of those showed up, they redoubled their efforts.

Sure, we moderns laugh and shake our heads at that primitive way of thinking. And yet millions of Americans who consider organized religion no better than a superstitious vestige of a prerational age nonetheless start searching for virgins to sacrifice every opportunity they get. While prominent doomsayers like Robert Kennedy Jr. and Barbra Streisand no longer walk around with sandwich boards proclaiming "the end is nigh," their message is still the same, no matter that facts, as in science, tend toward the other side.

For example, since the year 2000, greenhouse gas emissions, including carbon dioxide, are down nearly 1 percent in the United States. That's a significant amount, but the good news there, like the good news in Iraq and Peoria, is apparently lost on those whose career and ego interests lie in fear-thumping tales of imminent damnation. They probably wouldn't appreciate the reference to hellfire-and-brimstone preachers, but it's entirely apt.

And just as thousands of years ago a certain number of the populace made a very nice living by auditioning virgins and choosing babies for the fires, so, too, do we have our high priests and priestesses of doom—Paul Ehrlich, for example.

★ "The battle to feed all of humanity is over. In the 1970s and 1980s hundreds of millions of people will starve to death in spite of any crash programs embarked upon now. At this late date nothing can prevent a substantial increase in the world death rate."

Such was the gloomy prediction of the world's most famous environmental biologist in his 1968 book *The Population Bomb*, a mega-bestseller that blamed increased birthrates around the world for imminent catastrophes and called for immediate legislation to begin controlling birthrates worldwide (like adding contraceptives to the food supply).

"A minimum of ten million people, most of them children, will starve to death during each year of the 1970s," Ehrlich wrote. "But this is a mere handful compared to the numbers that will be starving before the end of the century."

Ehrlich was hardly alone in his doomsday predictions, and with his stature as a respected author, lecturer, and full professor at Stanford, he soon gained millions of adherents.

But in fact, the last years of the twentieth century and first few of the twenty-first were remarkable for exactly the opposite: the reduction of famine deaths. While one death from starvation is of course one too many, the roughly 2 million deaths in 1999 and since were a historical anomaly—and could reasonably be blamed on politics more than lack of food, what with warlords and despots hording and reselling food supplies intended for the needy. Compare, for example, the end of the twentieth century with the end of the nineteenth, when 25 million people died of famine-related causes in a world that had only half the present population.

But being wrong, even grotesquely wrong, didn't deter Ehrlich. He continued to write books all through the 1970s and '80s predicting even greater catastrophes that were avoidable only if governments took immediate steps—like mandating a limit on the number of children born to each couple. What's interesting is that modern-day Western Europe now finds itself living in a kind of Ehrlichville, and enduring its consequences, even if he himself wasn't directly responsible. For years now, the mostly secular countries of that continent—France, Germany, Holland, Italy—freed from the biblical exhortation to multiply, have seen their birthrates plummet far below "replacement rate," meaning that more people die than are born, sending their societies into a kind of death spiral, with not enough new bodies working to support the vast cradle-to-grave mechanisms of their socialist societies. They now have to "import" workers from other countries—mostly Islamic countries, where there's an unending supply of unemployed.

Unfortunately for Europe, those workers, by and large, are less interested in assimilating into, say, French culture than they are in maintaining their Islamic identity and sending home paychecks. The roosting-chickens consequence of that—no doubt a small glimpse into a dark future—came in the fall of 2005, when rampaging Muslim "youths," as the news media named them, rioted in Paris and its suburbs. So my advice to you, if you have a soft spot for the Paris or Rome you once visited, is to go back now and take your camera. Because in a few years, it could be gone—the French flag replaced by a star and crescent hanging from the Arc de Triomphe.

My favorite Ehrlich tale of caution began in 1980, when he famously accepted a bet offered by economist Julian Simon. Simon laughingly disagreed with Ehrlich's insistence that the world would suffer from massive shortages of critical natural resources, and he declared that the market price of any five metals would actually decline by the year 1990, which is to say that they would be more, not less, plentiful.

Ehrlich got the pleasure and honor of choosing the five metals, so he picked copper, chrome, nickel, tin, and tungsten out of the belief that they were at least as likely as any other metals to become more scarce and therefore more expensive— no doubt thanks to human rapaciousness and ecological catastrophe; this was, after all, the decade in which our scientific End of Days scenario was destined to occur.

But, as Simon had predicted, every one of those five metals cost less in 1990 than it had in 1980—by an astounding average of nearly 40 percent.

Nonetheless, Ehrlich is still a "distinguished" professor at Stanford, still writing books about overpopulation, overconsumption, and imminent catastrophe—and is still considered by those in the media elite to be a genius whose predictions should be taken seriously. Obviously, calamities do happen sometimes, as September 11 and Hurricane Katrina proved. But those were by and large man-made catastrophes: man's evil, in the case of September 11, and man's lack of common sense and preparation, in the case of Katrina. In general, large-scale catastrophes are the exception, not the rule, in Western developed nations with sensible building codes. In our neck of the woods, only the tiniest fraction of the doomsday scenarios we've heard and believed have actually come to pass. Our experts have been mistaken so frequently, and sometimes so spectacularly, that if we had any sense at all we'd stop listening to them and start heeding our innate good judgment—for instance, getting out of New Orleans before the storm hits instead of waiting for an "expert" or a government official to tell us what to do.

True, it's hard to turn a deaf ear to those cries, given the screaming meemies of the media's pervasive influence in our lives. I remember last year when the *Today* show's Matt Lauer interviewed soldiers in Iraq and refused to believe that they felt so gung-ho about their mission. He asked, "What would you say to those who are doubtful that morale can be that high?"

"Sir," said one of them, "if I got my news from the newspapers also, I'd be pretty depressed as well."

Wise words indeed. That American soldier was in a position to see firsthand that the war was going far better than the press had been reporting.

Most of us, however, are somewhat more defenseless against the constant harping. Yet even if we can't tune out the naysaying, we can at least arm ourselves with the kind of knowledge that helps to put their cries of wolf into perspective.

The Gulf War is a perfect example. On August 2, 1990, several divisions of Iraqi troops invaded and overran Kuwait, sparking an international crisis. In response, U.S. President George H. W. Bush orchestrated a thirty-eight-nation coalition of air and ground troops, more than half a million in all, and based them in Saudi Arabia in preparation for a counteroffensive intended to drive Iraq out of Kuwait. With the American president calling the shots, and the military led by an American general, Norman Schwarzkopf, this was to be an essentially American war—the country's first military confrontation of the post–Cold War era and its first truly substantial fighting since Vietnam.

Believing that Americans still suffered a hangover from Vietnam and would do anything to avoid seeing its young men come home in body bags again, Iraqi leader Saddam Hussein defiantly refused to withdraw his troops from Kuwait and in fact promised that the fighting would amount to "the mother of all battles."

Soon came similar predictions from pundits and "experts." Either we would suffer a Vietnam-like "quagmire" or endure hundreds of thousands of dead—or both. The network news anchors, all of whom had covered Vietnam personally, used the "Q" word repeatedly and broadcast the estimates of military "analysts" who concluded that the young U.S. troops were no match for the "battle-hardened" (they'd fought Iran for eight years) Iraqis.

On National Public Radio, Scott Simon suggested that the treads might fall off American tanks in the desert, that a hit-and-run guerilla war would be waged by the "wily" Iraqis who knew the desert a lot better than we did, and that to win, the Allies would essentially have to carpet bomb the country. On PBS, Mark Shields spoke for millions when he suggested, as a war veteran himself, that there was nothing at issue in the Gulf worth the rivers of American blood that were sure to flow.

Other prognosticators—presumed "experts" in Arab affairs—envisioned the entire Arab world (the "Arab street") rising up to fight not the Iraqis but the usurpers. In short, the scenario was an unmitigated disaster: massive rebellions in each of the twenty-two Arab countries, Americans and American soldiers slaughtered by locals in the streets of Riyadh, airliners blown out of the sky with handheld artillery, and rich sheikhs running out of their villas to lob Molotov cocktails at Westerners. The price of oil in Texas? At least a hundred dollars a barrel.

Meanwhile, environmentalists predicted that deliberately set oil fires in Kuwait would create such air pollution that the sun would be all but blotted out of the sky—in essence, nuclear winter. Physicist Carl Sagan ran computer models and said that "the net effects will be very similar to the explosion of the Indonesian volcano Tambora in 1815, which resulted in the year 1816 being known as the year without a summer." He insisted that the resulting soot and plumes would wreak havoc on the monsoon patterns in Asia, shutting off rains and leaving hundreds of millions with nothing to harvest.

After a nearly five-month run-up to war, Allied planes began pounding Baghdad and surrounding areas in mid-January of 1991, using sophisticated technology to drop millions of pounds of munitions over the following five weeks. Only then did ground troops advance, first routing Iraqi troops out of Kuwait and then chasing them into Iraq. Iraqis and Iraqi soldiers were so demoralized, and happy to see Western faces, that they usually surrendered without a fight—some of them to journalists. The ground war lasted only a hundred hours before Saddam Hussein agreed to surrender—and on that day, in millions of homes across America, the quarterly newsletter of the environmental group Greenpeace arrived in mailboxes. "As we go to press," an editorial said, "a bloody and protracted ground war has begun." (Apparently, Greenpeace's crystal ball had an air pollution problem, and their editors some credibility issues.)

In all, there were 184 American fatalities.

Now, how does this apply to our current war? Actually, the situations are somewhat analogous. Mere days after we launched the invasion of Afghanistan in the fall of 2002, the media were already using the word "quagmire" to describe the situation, believing that American armed forces would face defeat in the craggy mountains of that desolate country, just as previous empires throughout history had, the most recent of which had been the Soviet Union. But, oops, we overthrew the Taliban in a matter of weeks, and soon thereafter the formerly brutalized Afghanis elected a democratic government. True, we still have troops there, and may for a long time, but anyone who suggests that the trade-off wasn't worth it is living in a utopian fantasy, not the real world.

Meanwhile, many of the same people who claimed we couldn't win in Iraq the first time, and in Afghanistan a decade later, predicted that there would be hundreds of thousands dead from the 2003 invasion to overthrow Saddam Hussein, thanks to the chemical and biological weapons that he was bound to launch (and which they now say they knew he didn't have all along). Hussein stayed barely longer than his statues did, and in 2005 alone the Iraqi people defied the Islamo-fascists who are the real enemy and voted three times to establish authentic democracy in a country—and culture—that has never known it.

Yes, and sadly, we have lost a few thousand of our finest young people. But here again, anyone who argues that the cost is far too high is both ignorant of history (our losses are historically low) and disdainful of our brave soldiers, Marines, pilots, and sailors who don't want to leave until the war is won.

Maybe if the "expert" naysayers would stop looking for signs of the defeat that they predict anew each morning, they'd see the same evidence of winning progress that our fighting forces do.

And maybe it would help us keep our equilibrium if we kept in mind that it was Hitler who originated the "Big Lie" theory—the idea that the masses of people are far more likely to believe a colossal untruth than a small one. In other words, just because a prediction is terrifying and unlikely doesn't make it probable.

My friend at the factory—so worried about the bird flu epidemic when it wasn't even on the horizon that he began stockpiling drugs that weren't even designed to protect against it—would do well to remember a simple bit of wisdom proved repeatedly throughout history: To err is human, but to be really really wrong, you have to be an expert.

A TRIBUTE TO EZRA POUND'S "IN A STATION OF THE METRO"

★   ★   ★

In the beginning, it was still. And then Satan invented the leaf blower. Enough said.

LIFE EXPERIENCE FOR SALE

★　★　★

In a corner of my living room stands a Fender Stratocaster electric guitar, a generous gift courtesy of the people at Fender, given to me when my TV show filmed at their factory in 2005. Marked and scarred both front and back, it looks like it's been through several tours of duty in the rock and roll wars. Did Hendrix knock out "Foxy Lady" on it? Clapton play a sizzling "Layla"? Or maybe Springsteen blistered through "Born to Run."

Actually, none of those guitar legends ever touched it. Nor has my neighbor's head-banging teenager, Karma, who plays in a grunge band. In fact, no one has ever plunked a single note or formed a chord on those virgin strings.

So where did the battle scars come from? The Fender factory—by workers trained to distress fresh-off-the-floor guitars and make them look like they'd already played sold-out stadiums on a world tour. I watched them do it myself, and idly imagined getting a job at the Corvette plant in Bowling Green, Ohio, to put dings in new cherry-red turbos hot off the line. What ended that wonderful daydream was remembering that we still like our cars to look clean and unused—unlike, apparently, our guitars. And jeans.

What does that mean about us? Let's see.

Back in the '60s, when ordinary people who didn't know the top side of a saddle or the useful end of a hammer began wearing jeans every day as a fashion/cultural statement, there was really only one brand of jean to choose from—Levis 501s. They seemed to last forever, which was a good thing for a couple of reasons. First, because when they were new, they were as stiff as cardboard, uncomfortable, and kind of embarrassing to wear. That dark blue original color and funny crease that wouldn't disappear till maybe the twentieth wash screamed, "Look at me, I'm new!"—which was the last sound you wanted to hear from them. Which was why some people would get a new pair and spend the day in the Laundromat, washing them time after time after time (oh, and they also shrunk about 10 percent over the first few drying cycles, so when you bought them, you had to plan accordingly). One guy I knew, who had a little money when I didn't, paid another guy I knew to wear his new jeans for the first several months to break them in. He needed the money more than he minded the chore or the embarrassment of looking so uncool.

Wearing the same pair of jeans every day over the years, you and your jeans became like best friends. Putting them on was a confident pleasure, like climbing into a hot tub, and you got attached to them in a way that you would never feel about another article of clothing—which was the second good reason why they seemed to last forever. No wonder Donovan sang an ode to jeans "that you feel so groovy in," or that the song was a big hit.

Those jeans had earned your love, and you'd earned theirs.

As far as love affairs go, this one was utterly requited. And deserved. And destined to last until death did you part, yours or its. When you walked down the street, you and your jeans said something about each other—that you'd been places together, lived life, had adventures, knew stuff, were cool. Or so it seemed . . . until somebody somewhere came up with the idea of "prewashed" jeans to make them appear "preworn" (hey, maybe it was the guy who paid the other guy to break his in). Suddenly, any Ward Cleaver who'd been wearing tweed slacks while teaching Beaver to box could now strut like he'd spent the last two years on a Eurasian backpacking trip. And then jeans as a symbol of anything that jeans were supposed to symbolize had become ruined.

Now blue jeans are standard issue in every American closet and worn in place of suits to Broadway plays. They're no longer the exclusive province of American companies, and authentic Levis, which thirty years ago you couldn't wear on a Paris street without a dozen people asking if they could buy them for ten— even twenty—times what you paid, closed down its American plants and struggles to keep up with its imitators.

Worse, designers have gotten into the business of not just making jeans but of charging to rip them up and sell them as "distressed," which is actually the word that comes to mind when you see the price tag: more than my first car, if not yours, too. And for what? Tearing holes in the knees. Fraying the bottoms.

At the risk of sounding suspiciously like a cranky old fart (or a creaky one), there's something not quite right about that, though I guess I should've seen the writing on the wall years back, when people began ironing their jeans; now they even have them dry cleaned, distressed or not. ("Listen, I know when I brought these in, they had more holes and tears than they do now. You fixed them, didn't you? Well, you're going to have to pay to have them re-ripped, or buy me a new torn pair.")

It strikes me, in a way, as akin to wearing someone else's military medals—no, better, a used army jacket. The image you communicate is, let's face it, at least vaguely disingenuous, if not dishonest.

Same with leather jackets. It used to take years to get that buttery softness, and those cracks that each told a story, and that look that said, "This is mine, damn it, and I broke it in, and I'm proud, and I'm gonna wear it forever." Now, hanging on the rack in the store is that same jacket with those same cracks and same feel. Talk about ready to wear. What do they do, get some unemployed Hell's Angels as jacket busters?

What I liked about the old days, I can see now in retrospect, is that you could actually tell by someone's clothes whether he or she had been there and done that. Now, pencil pushers dress like Indiana Jones, and nobody who doesn't know better knows better (at least you can still tell something by the hands—that is, until some entrepreneur comes up with paste-on calluses).

While there's obviously nothing dangerous or insidious about buying clothes that make it hard to tell just who's come back from Skull Island after wrestling a giant gorilla into the hold of a ship, it still seems somehow inauthentic: the triumph of style over substance.

Given the rate at which science and technology are advancing, someday we may be able to buy experiences, as it were, by downloading someone else's memories directly into our own brains. We'll call them "bio data," and charge by the length and quality, with Steven Jobs setting up an Apple iMemories Store. Then what? Will those memories be considered any less legitimate than the ones we've actually lived through? I can't see why they would be, not with the worlds of filmed entertainment and virtual reality nearly merging now. Who would object? Only Luddites and traditionalists, of whom there aren't many left anyway.

Even so, when the day of that capability comes, I probably won't sign up to share any of my memories with the adventure-challenged, nor will I be eager to absorb parts of someone else's life as my own. Not unless—wait a second, yes, I can see it—it's some rock star's memory of standing on stage in front of twenty thousand screaming fans (lighted candles optional).

Better, maybe that memory will come with both talent and skill attached. Then I'd have something legitimate to do with that beautiful guitar of mine besides just admire it from afar. It would be great to add my own dings and belt marks to the ones already there.

IN PRAISE OF FAILURE

★　★　★

If the factory we're visiting is in a small town, as many of
them are, there's a pretty good chance that a local newspaper
reporter will come out to interview me for a feature story about
the show. It's somewhat of a curiosity when a television show
comes to town, and, if the newspaper covers entertainment
anyway, as most do nowadays, those column inches will have
more relevance for the locals than whatever the Associated
Press or *New York Times* happens to be offering for reprint that
day. Which is why I like talking to local reporters, just as I enjoy
promoting the show a few times a month on radio stations
across the country.

Those radio interviews are called "phoners," meaning that
the host will call me at the prearranged time and we'll chat for
about ten minutes or so, ostensibly about the show. Naturally,
though, most hosts either want to know or think their listeners
want to know the latest news about Cliff and the other ex-
Cheers members, so sooner or later they'll ask the same questions I've heard since that show went off the air.

For years I tried to answer such questions truthfully—that

we're all still friends and enjoy each other's company whenever we see each other, and that, like people who long ago worked in the same insurance office, for example, we don't necessarily hang out regularly together anymore. But I found that that frequently wasn't juicy enough for the questioners. They'd push for details, details, details about who was doing what with whom where—that is, gossip. So at last I realized I could move on much faster, and avoid their insinuations that I was sitting on some really good dirt, by answering this way: "Ted? Oh, yeah, we're playing golf in about an hour." "Kirstie? Yeah, she and Rhea and George and I are playing Yahtzee." "Shelley? Oh, too bad, you just missed her. We're practicing our tap-dance routine for the Easter pageant."

For *John Ratzenberger's Made in America*, I always try to respond as if I've never been asked a particular question before, even if it's obvious, and even if I have. Like: "What's your show about?"

Most of the time I'll say, "It's a celebration of American manufacturing and ingenuity," or words to that effect.

What's interesting is that the small-town reporters who live near what's likely to be at least one factory—the one my crew and I have come to see—don't need to follow up that question in order to clarify my meaning. To them, the words are plainly self-evident. But to radio hosts in bigger cities, who may or may not have ever been inside a factory, let alone worked in one, my answer is rarely sufficient. Those guys tend to ask a follow-up that requires connecting more dots about companies moving their production facilities offshore, and what the loss of manufacturing jobs has done to America both economically and spiritually.

Even so, I was not prepared for this follow-up from the host of a big-city radio show: "What do you mean by celebration?"

The question took me by surprise; at first I didn't understand his insinuation. I remember thinking, *What do you mean, what do I mean?* So, half a beat behind his cynicism, I answered as if the word "celebration" was one of those twenty-five-cent words rarely uttered by ordinary people.

"Well," I said, "we highlight the companies and people who do whatever it takes to still turn out the best products in the world. I suppose you could say that we *celebrate*"—hitting the word hard, for emphasis—"that they have the determination and skill to keep their factories open against the odds, and that the people who work there take pride in what they do. It's kind of a salute to creativity, resourcefulness, and the Protestant work ethic."

"Huh," he said, but it was really a harrumph. "I'm not sure that's anything to celebrate."

And then, without missing a beat, he went on to ask about when I'd last seen the *Cheers* cast.

After the interview, I hung up the phone and turned on the news. The big story under discussion was that morning drive-time radio host Howard Stern had decided to leave broadcast radio, which falls under the moderate language and decorum restrictions imposed by the Federal Communications Commission, and move to satellite radio, which doesn't—for $100 million a year.

Huh? Had I heard right? A hundred mill?

Yes, for five years. Minimum. The new satellite company was betting the house that a hundred million dollars a year would buy them a billion dollars a year's worth of subscribers eager to hear an even raunchier Howard Stern, expletives no longer deleted, sex fantasies no longer constrained.

What occurred to me was that Stern had built his success as the pied piper of failure. He made a career out of mocking the standards of Western civilization. He was the poster boy—well, one of many in popular culture—for a celebration of failure as a lifestyle choice.

I was still shaking my head when, coincidentally, on came a commercial for a hamburger chain, except this didn't look like any hamburger commercial I'd ever seen. It starred tabloid celebrity Paris Hilton—a girl famous for being famous, her fame mostly achieved on the back, so to speak, of her Internet sex video, and by her total lack of modesty, which she reestablishes nearly every time she goes out in public. That is to say, it was a commercial that celebrated our entire culture of failure. A cynical grab for our attention centered on someone who has achieved nothing other than our attention. In it, she enters a garage wearing a plunging leather outfit and proceeds to suds herself and a Bentley with a hose—well, you get the idea.

Mainstream American popular culture, seen most clearly in comedy and music, has shifted perceptibly away from honoring success and progress in favor of defeat and cynicism, the twin pillars of failure. That would be a sad development were it not so terrifying—indicative of a society in need of what we now call an intervention. And for the same reason, by the way: to prevent self-destruction. While I don't for a minute believe that most Americans embrace negativity, the popular culture to which we're all exposed and from which none of us can be insulated now turns to failure as a source of humor and musical inspiration. Which means that it's sooner or later bound to affect us all.

The comedian George Carlin is as talented and sharp as any comedian of the last half century. But in the past few years George has sadly abandoned healthy skepticism, his former stock in trade, in favor of cynicism and defeatism. From where I sit, the act that used to crack me up now sounds far more bitter than witty, as though he's been listening to too much Howard Stern.

You can see that for yourself if you get HBO, for which Carlin has done several one-man shows over the years. In the early ones, his observational takes were gut-splittingly funny—focused, for the most part, on language ("Before they invented drawing boards, what did they go back to?"), as well as on idiocy and idiots (class clowns, television news anchors, drug users, etc.). But in a special recorded not long before 9/11, he actually commended terrorists and school shooters. And in his special from 2005, he praised, among other things, disasters like wildfires—insisting (or pretending to insist) that he always roots for them to grow bigger and more destructive. Even coming from George, it's pretty shocking stuff, and I contend that whether you think he's funny now—as his huge audience that night appeared to—depends on whether you've embraced defeat and despair as the new status quo.

Rare, these days, is the comedian who hasn't; and rare is the comic who doesn't work blue, as we used to say, meaning that his language is peppered—or marinated—with vulgarisms. (Jerry Seinfeld, Ellen DeGeneres, and Sinbad are three that I can think of who don't swear on stage.) Back when, working blue was something lesser comedians did because those words got cheap laughs, like mother-in-law jokes; they were the entertainment equivalent of shooting fish in a barrel.

Today's crop of comedians believes that swearing makes them authentic, a reflection of the culture that celebrates cynicism and failure. That's a far different attitude than when Rodney Dangerfield made himself the joke's butt instead of this country ("A girl phoned the other day and said, 'Come on over. Nobody's home.' I went over. Nobody was home." "My wife made me join a bridge club. I jump off next Tuesday."). Seeing "David Spade tear 2005 a new one," in the words of Comedy Central's promo for his year-end special, isn't my idea of funny, but it's sure the kind of anything-goes cynicism that encourages morons like the young idiot who showed up at the vice president's post-Katrina press conference in Mississippi and shouted, "Go f--- yourself, Mr. Cheney."

You see the same awful attitude in gangsta rap and hip-hop. To me, "rap music" is an oxymoron, but my beef isn't with the "music" itself; it's with the lyrics, like those on Eminem's "'97 Bonnie and Clyde," in which the rapper explains to his young daughter as they drive why he slit Mommy's throat (because she made him angry), stuffed her in the trunk of the car, and plans to dump her in the lake. "There goes mama, spwashin' in the wa-ta."

Nice, huh?

And here's one of the other preeminent rappers of the day, Kanye West (of "George Bush doesn't care about black people" fame), in the immortal "We Don't Care," an ode to easy cash: "And all my people that's drug dealin' jus' to get by / Stack ya money till it gets sky."

Fascinating.

But compared to many rap "songs," these are somewhat tame. Many are more in-your-face with both messages and language, and drip contempt in every line.

But of course, contempt and disrespect are the whole point of hip-hop culture, which itself permeates every corner of popular culture, including a new reading genre called "street lit" that glamorizes black criminals. Professional athletes even adopt hip-hop attitudes and clothing, as do movie stars, some of whom (Colin Farrell, for example) dress like they're auditioning for an inner-city production of *Yo, Hamlet* (which may not be such a bad idea).

Watch the MTV awards show sometime if you want to see successful, rich, mainstream entertainers competing to be cool enough with an audience that apparently believes standard English is hopelessly lame and out-of-date. Kelly Clarkson, the first *American Idol*, bantering on stage with the rapper Ludacris, actually moaned, "Oh God, I'm so white."

Gee, here I'd thought the goal was to get past skin color as a determinant of anything other than how high an SPF you need. But apparently that's considered a pre-postmodern attitude in popular culture—meaning it's obsolete. Apparently standard English is now considered uncool, unhip, geeky. Go figure. Believe me, it's a real eye opener to Google "feel so white" and see that most of the *few thousand* hits that come up are lamentations of people mortified at not being cool enough among hip-hop African Americans—which strikes me as so undeniably racist and condescending that I'm embarrassed for anybody who feels that way, and curious why blacks put up with that kind of patronizing. (Reminds me of the scene in the movie *Silver Streak* when Richard Pryor tries to teach Gene Wilder, shoe polish on his face, to get down.) No wonder Bill Cosby has been so adamant about the need to de-glorify hip-hop, which is the media's dominant image of American blacks despite the fact that it represents only a tiny minority.

Meanwhile, "feel so black" yields only a *few hundred* hits, most of them referring to "black and blue," not skin color, and none of them, at least that I could find, referring to someone black feeling out of place among whites.

But what are we to make of this when "acting white" is a term some African Americans use contemptuously for other blacks who either study hard in school or work hard on the job? What's the message, if "acting white" is as uncool as "feeling white"? Well, Cosby for one is mortified by what he sees as the message. As am I. As is everyone of good will who believes that we're all—black and white and brown and polka-dot—inextricably linked as a nation, and that anything that weakens a single link weakens everyone.

Describing how hip-hop culture came to be so influential is something best left to qualified sociologists, but I suspect it has something to do with reflecting a worldview that was already embedded in the mainstream. Call it the "Jerry Springerization" of America, after the man who revels in giving fifteen minutes of fame to thousands of people who, for most of history and until not that long ago, would've been ashamed to show up in public, let alone on national TV, wearing dirty underwear—on their heads.

Talk about weakening the nation.

But of course, why wouldn't they parade shamelessly in front of the cameras? After all, they see the world portrayed every day as a plugged toilet by elite Americans who would never think of themselves as living in the same sewer as Jerry Springer. I'm talking about the mainstream press.

Choose any front-page story, on any given day, in the *New York Times*, the *Washington Post*, the *Los Angeles Times*, et al., or any top-of-the-broadcast story on the big-three network news shows. What you'll read/hear is that something's wrong; and not just wrong, but terribly wrong. Even when it's right. The economy, for example. No amount of good news is good enough for reporters to write, "Things are going swimmingly." Interest rates could be down, home ownership at an all-time high, home equity in the tens of trillions of dollars, unemployment at historical lows, and the economy growing at an excellent 4 percent—which, come to think of it, described our economy throughout most of 2005 and the beginning of 2006—and the majority of reporters will, in the first paragraph, include the obligatory "Yes, but," which sometimes comes in the form of, "To be sure." These qualifiers let us know that no matter how good it seems, you're deluded if you think so, and they're followed by a quote from the one nervous-nellie analyst on Wall Street who sees dark clouds on the horizon filled with the acid rain of imminent depression. (Sample *New York Times* headline from early this year: "U.S. Gains 108,000 More Jobs, but Pace of Growth Slows.")

It's a glorification of failure, of despair, of hopelessness.

No wonder more than half the country at any given time these days believes that we're suffering in a recession, even though the people polled admit that they themselves are doing great, as are their neighbors. What they read and hear, apparently, is more powerful than what they experience and see with their own eyes.

Take the war in Iraq. If you read/listen to only the mainstream press, you'd never know that Iraqis themselves, according to every poll taken, are overwhelmingly hopeful about their future; or that they're enjoying a vibrant and free press for the first time; or that their infrastructure is being quickly rebuilt and improved; or that for most of two years now they've been governed successfully at the local level by elected officials; or that Iraq's economy is growing; or that the country's citizens don't want our troops to leave before the job is complete; or that re-up levels for American military personnel who have *actually served in Iraq and seen what's going on there* are at historical highs; or any of a hundred—make that a thousand—good-news stories about the war and its progress. (And some people wondered why the Pentagon was paying Iraqi journalists to get out the news.)

The mainstream press's reportage of Iraq and the economy is typical, in that it reflects a belief that reporting facts when the facts are good is unforgivably Pollyannaish, and therefore not authentic "news." Like hip-hop culture, like all the Jerry Springers out there, the press's portrait of what's happening at any given moment in our country reflects the rather skewed impression of the human anatomy to which the average proctologist eventually gets accustomed. No matter that our news purveyors believe they're being faithful to the truth—and I'll give them that. By zooming in so closely on negativity, they leave no room in the frame for good news. So what they give us is essentially a lie, and what they breed in us is cynicism.

I'm reminded of a *San Francisco Chronicle* photograph I saw in the last year or so, taken at an antiwar rally, of a child wearing a bandana that said "People of color say no to war." Anyone looking at that photo would've concluded what I did about this girl's idealistic hope that war be banished from the earth. Well, as it turned out, the photo had been cropped to tell a completely different story from the truth. In fact, the girl—as another photographer on the scene chronicled—was one of a contingent of young people, all wearing Hamas-like clothes and bandanas, holding up vulgar signs . . . and taking direction from a woman wearing a T-shirt emblazoned with the Communist flag of Vietnam. So while the original photo run by the *Chronicle* was, strictly speaking, true, the story it told was actually a lie.

No, most news isn't as blatantly falsified as that. But there's falsified and there's falsified. For instance, if a tree falls in the forest and the *New York Times* doesn't report it, most people don't know it fell, since the majority of the mainstream media take their marching orders from the *Times*. And if the tree's falling actually was reported, but on page A31, then it must not have been a consequential tree death. Anyway, that's how it ends up working, because most people instinctively ascribe greater importance to what makes the front pages than they do to stories buried inside.

So the question is, what are the criteria for deciding what gets reported and where? The answer, it seems to me, has everything to do with the same cynicism that drove the *Chronicle* photographer to either crop his photo that way or not protest when the photo editor did; it's a worldview more comfortable with America's failures than its successes. Frankly, I don't see this point as even arguable, given how the press reported one of the biggest stories of the last many years—the multiple elections in Iraq and Afghanistan.

In the scheme of things, those elections could not have been more significant—they showed that both countries, after five thousand years (and in the case of Afghanistan, stone-age amenities), had begun the long journey toward self-government as democracies. And yet, none of the elections were given the prominence they deserved, especially compared to the utter non-story about former ambassador Joseph Wilson's CIA wife and Niger uranium and "leaks" in the White House. Wilson's now-infamous *New York Times* op-ed, intended to discredit the

Bush administration's reasons for going to war, was ironically filled with lies and factual inaccuracies, as the 9/11 Commission would later show, but that did little to diminish Wilson's credibility with the press. Why? Well, it seems to me that the answer has something to do with which story paints a picture of America as successful and which as a failure.

America's failure was the subtext of two other huge non-stories of the recent past: the Abu Ghraib prison "torture" scandal and the Koran "flushing" at the Guantanamo Bay prison compound for enemy combatants. You could almost hear the press celebrating as they quoted opposition candidates and citizens decrying how a few Americans mistreated and humiliated a few prisoners in Iraq. Missing, of course, from their reports was any mention of the room in that prison where Saddam Hussein used to leak acid on his prisoners, to make them die slowly, in agony; or of the giant shredders into which innocents used to be tossed feet first; or the rape rooms or starvation chambers or any of two dozen grotesque tortures Saddam and his minions devised for the sadistic subjugation of his people.

Then, too, in all the bloodletting over our alleged "desecration" of a "holy" Koran down a Gitmo toilet, a few facts seemed to elude *Newsweek* and its journalistic colleagues: one, that America had given that Koran to the prisoner; two, that using words like "holy Koran" and "desecrate" in apparent sincerity, without quotation marks, was grotesquely ironic for reporters who believe that a portrait of the Virgin Mary with cow dung on it is art; three, that to even possess a Christian Bible in countries like Saudi Arabia is a crime punishable by death; and four, that, well, it's physically impossible to flush even a few pieces of paper, let alone an entire book, down one of those toilets. No matter. The narrative fit the theme in the same way that myth becomes fact.

Defeat is the mainstream culture's operative norm. In other times, a public pronouncement by the leader of one of our two major political parties that a war we're fighting is unwinnable would have brought such a loud din of condemnation that he would have been forced to resign in shame. But when Howard Dean, chairman of the Democratic National Committee, told a Texas (of all places) radio audience, "The idea that we're going to win the war in Iraq is just plain wrong," the biggest newspapers in the country either ignored the remark or did day-after stories that discussed the possible political fallout. Some even gave more prominence to his claims that he'd been quoted "out of context" than they had to the remarks themselves, when in fact what he said had been recorded and reported accurately.

That din of condemnation? Barely a whisper, only briefly, and then it was back to business. Why? Maybe because he had so much company, starting with those who believe the war had already been lost, like House Minority Leader Nancy Pelosi, and Congressman John Murtha, a man who'd left college fifty-five years ago in order to join the Marines and fight in Korea. When people that prominent consider victory unachievable for the United States, you know that this is not your father's America. Your father had Betty Grable, your children have Paris Hilton. Your father had Jack Benny, your children have Howard Stern.

In this America, defeat and failure are no crime, and the only shame is to feel shame. So every parent gets to drive around with a bumper sticker declaring that his kid was student of the month, never thinking it through to realize that if *every* kid is special, then *no* kid is special.

And that's how the honoring of failure begins—by not honoring success.

No doubt my radio interviewer, who didn't understand what there was to celebrate about America's factories, won't get it either when democratic Iraq replaces France on the UN Security Council. But I'll cut him some slack, since that monumental event might not even make the news.

We really do have it made in America. But for how much longer, if we don't get back to honoring success and not changing its definition to glorify failure?

PACK RAT NATION

★ ★ ★

I learn a lot at the factories we visit, and not just about how to build things. For instance, I'd never before heard of the concept called just-in-time manufacturing until we took our cameras into an Ohio plant where executives explained that they excelled at limiting production of component parts to a maximum of two days' worth of inventory in order to keep costs down and profits up. One of the managers pointed to a former warehouse, once used to hold inventory, that they were converting to additional factory space in order to handle the orders that they never could've handled before adopting the just-in-time program.

Coincidentally, when I got home from that trip I received an e-mail from a friend who'd decided with his wife to do something adventurous that winter and rent a two-bedroom house on Nantucket with another couple, just to shake things up a bit. The e-mail was full of details about how interesting it was to find himself in a sort of encounter group by virtue of living so closely with two people who weren't family. But what really got my attention was his passing comment about how shocked he was to discover how little stuff he really needed to live; and that now he couldn't stop thinking about what he wanted to do the moment he returned to his big mountaintop home in North Carolina: "I'm already planning a huge bonfire for all of the boxes of stuff that are in my attic that I haven't opened since we moved there ten years ago. And everything that I haven't seen, worn, or used in the last year will be given away to charity. And that's almost everything in there! Let me at it."

I understand what he meant. Boy, do I—more than he could've imagined when he wrote those words. For years I would look at my disordered garage, feel sick to my stomach, put on a sweatshirt and some jeans . . . and then realize how much I needed a root canal, or to finish that Swedish land-use study I'd been avoiding since the Dukakis nomination. In other words, I preferred doing anything to cleaning up that mess. At the same time, I was paying for storage lockers filled with junk and other assorted memorabilia that I hadn't seen, let alone touched, since the early 1980s. Oh, and my attic was crammed to the rafters with tons of debris that I may never have used, let alone wanted; the whole space was like a colossal dumpster.

So was my brain, it seemed. Thoughts were cluttered, disorganized, hard to find. One year during my annual checkup, I finally asked my doctor if he had any ideas about what was going on with me. A brain tumor, maybe? He was skeptical but I insisted, so he ran some tests and, of course, found nothing wrong organically. Then came his diagnosis:

"Welcome to middle age," he said.

Except that wasn't my problem. Not nearly. In fact, I only discovered the problem and solution by accident, when I sold my home and moved, which forced me at long last to clean out the attic and garage at the same time as my storage lockers.

The problem, apparently, was my attic. And garage. And storage lockers. They were filled. For. No. Good. Reason. With junk. Junk that was clogging my thoughts, heart, and my soul like some sort of weird voodoo.

Except that it wasn't voodoo. It was physics—mental physics.

Psychically, owning all that stuff to no good purpose must have weighed on me. Every time I contemplated all those extraneous belongings tucked away here and there, I became aware of a vaguely sinister feeling, as though some irresistible force had invaded my brain—you know, a commie mind-control experiment, like in *The Manchurian Candidate*. In fact, I'm not sure I even had to actually contemplate those belongings to evoke the reaction; I think the feeling was there all the time in the form of low-level confusion—or at least ebbing powers of concentration.

Once I was able to think clearly again, I figured that out and formulated a theory. One's mind, I now postulate, is as organized or as cluttered as one's garage/closet/attic/car trunk.

That makes sense, doesn't it? The two act as mirror images of each other, with the physical space manifesting the mental one. Just as we tend to react to people, places, things, and situations in ways that are consistent with our personalities—which makes our reactions overall somewhat predictable—so do we relate to the physical universe the way we relate to the abstract one.

Those of us who acquire and store and forget about and jam into small spaces just one more thing—well, that's usually what we do with our thoughts, too. And those of us who are meticulously neat and organized with our stuff probably tend to think a little more clearly than the crammers. There's no doubt in my mind (now that I can tell the difference between my mind and doubt) that after I was able to walk into the garage and immediately find whatever I was looking for, my brain's filing cabinet began offering up its wares with greater accuracy.

Anyway, that's my theory and I'm sticking to it—because it's based not just on my experience, but also the experiences of others I know. And maybe even you. Think about what happens when you decide to straighten out your sock drawer: you pull it out and match up mismatched pairs, throw away singletons and those with holes, arrange everything nice and neat, and slide the drawer back in feeling pretty good. And that good feeling lasts about a second—or until you realize that the T-shirt drawer right below is an even bigger mess. So you slide it out and perform the same kind of triage, which gives you a momentary sense of satisfaction that disappears as soon as you see that your underwear drawer requires immediate attention; and you wonder how you could've possibly not noticed this before now. Same with the workout clothes drawer, and the pocket knife and cuff-link drawer.

At last your entire dresser is straightened, sorted, and streamlined—and, darn it, you have to admit that there's something genuinely therapeutic about knowing that everything's in its place. So therapeutic, in fact, that suddenly you imagine you can hear your closet shouting to you, "Hey, pal, over here."

Naturally, you answer its call. Then, once you complete the job—and get rid of the eight shirts, four trousers, and five pairs of shoes that you haven't worn since the Crimean War—you feel so great that the tractor pull of cleaning out the Dagwood drawer is too powerful to resist. Followed by the tool chest. And when you've finished with those, you become aware of how truly, well, fresh you feel, as though you'd just spring-cleaned yourself.

Which leads, inevitably, to the garage and then the attic and then the car trunk.

And when those are done and purged of extraneous debris, so, too, it seems, are your brain and heart and soul. Without question, you can tell the difference before and after in terms of how well you're able to think.

I have a friend who works at home, in an office bedroom near the back of the house. The man, I'm sure I can say without hurting his feelings, is a slob—not in appearance, just his environment. Papers are strewn everywhere, especially on the floor; books lie askew; clothes cover the sofa; electronic equipment circa the Beatles is heaped in the corners; and every inch of desktop is veiled by papers and documents that even he can't identify anymore.

Yet here's the irony: his wife is a professional organizer, meaning that she goes into people's homes and helps them make logical and aesthetic sense of their living and work spaces. For example, she'll begin in someone's office—like her husband's—by asking questions: What do you need most? What do you need least? What do you like to have around you in the way of toys and decorative items? And then she'll literally remake the space—moving things in and out, throwing stuff away, setting up elegantly simple filing systems—so that it now serves that person's purpose at work. (She does the same, by the way, with closets—throwing away, rehanging, refocusing, etc.)

Generally, she says, the day or so after she completes a job her clients will call her to blow kisses of praise. They claim they work better, faster, cleaner, and more efficiently—in part because everything has a place and they can see at a glance where it all belongs; and in part because they actually think better . . . which they attribute to the new office order.

You can see where this is going. For years she begged her husband to let her remake his office. She played him back phone messages from ecstatic clients and showed him thank-you letters and e-mails. But he always rebuffed her, insisting that he could only work in chaos—"Like my brain. I like things that way."

It drove her crazy, though, knowing that such a pathetic mess was behind the (usually) closed door. "Just let me try it," she begged. "If you don't like it, you can go back to the way it was. I'll even help you mess things up again."

No shot. He was adamant, likening neatness and order to Kryptonite, and claiming that his powers of concentration would disappear. "I won't be able to think," he declared. "We'll go bankrupt."

"I'll risk it," she said.

"No," he said. "No, no, no, no, no."

Then he made the mistake of leaving town on a three-day business trip. His wife later told me that on his first day gone she walked by his empty office five times with an urge to go in there and do the job anyway, and five times she fought temptation. But her willpower went only so far, and on the sixth time she surrendered. The job took seven hours without a break.

When my unsuspecting friend returned, he froze in the doorway and stood speechless for half a minute, jaw dropped, eyes scanning every inch. His wife, hiding sheepishly down the hall, kept waiting for shouts and screams. Instead, silence. After a while she mustered the courage to check in, to see whether the shock had killed him. On the contrary, he was sitting at the desk, working well and intently. So much for the power of chaos. That night at dinner he uttered the magic words: "I was wrong" and "I love it. Thank you." By the next day he'd added, "You know what? I think I think better."

If this story is representative, and I believe it is, our entire country may be suffering from a collective case of mental constipation. Why? Because the self-storage industry is apparently one of the fastest-growing and most profitable businesses we've got going now, with many hundreds of thousands of people, even millions, shelling out hundreds of bucks a month to warehouse their bonanzas of belongings that won't otherwise fit in their already SRO attics and garages.

Just think about that (if your garage is clean enough to do so): a gazillion tons of junk essentially swept under the collective carpet.

There's one stretch of freeway not far from my house outside Los Angeles that I've begun calling "the flea market," given how many couches, coffee tables, lamps, and other assorted stuff that must've fallen off already full pickup trucks on the way to where? Storage lockers? Probably. There are about a dozen storage sites right off that freeway within a ten-mile radius, so it's a pretty good bet that that's where they were going. I see the trucks all the time—pickups trying to defy the laws of physics, crammed full like they'd just left 1930s Oklahoma on the way to California with everything in the world that the family owns.

One word comes to mind: whatthehellarewethinking?

That's pretty close to the word that will come to the minds of our loved ones when we pass away and they're suddenly in charge of cleaning out our lockers and garages and attics and closets. The next words will then be "selfish," "stupid," "ridiculous," "useless," "waste," and "Salvation Army."

And who could blame them for thinking that? Leaving messes for our children (or next of kin) to clean up when we're gone is as selfish as creating budget deficits that the next generation of taxpayers has to pay off. That's why I think we should, as a nation, adopt a modified just-in-time version of consumption (and federal spending). Just as manufacturers who adopt that philosophy purchase or make a component only when they need it for production, we can limit ourselves to buying or acquiring only what we need by giving ourselves a set number of belongings—say, five hundred physical items (books not included, of course) unrelated to work, and one hundred (more for women) items of clothing. That probably means getting rid of a boatload right now, and then contemplating long and hard what you really need when you have the urge to buy something new, as well as what you can now give away (or sell) in order to make room for it.

I know, I know, the "one in, one out" rule is a silly idea, one that's as improbable as snow in Hawaii. But there's merit in becoming even a little conscious of what we already own and what we actually need every time we want something—and *before* we buy it. After all, keeping inventory down and profits up doesn't have to apply only to factories.

And, incidentally, it does snow in Hawaii.

THE POWER OF PRAYER

★   ★   ★

I love the sound of church bells pealing at the hour—especially noon, when they make music. No matter where I am or what I'm doing, rowing a boat or shining my shoes, when those bells ring within my earshot I always pause a little, readjust my attention, and enjoy the moment. But never did those bells sound more musical to me than on the day I was in a New England factory, north of my hometown, shooting the breeze with one of the workers while waiting for my TV crew to set up the next shot.

Ray, the worker, and I were off in a corner going on about this and that and how our high schools played ball against each other, and for some reason we got on the subject of children. (Well, not exactly "for some reason." If you're a parent you know you don't need a good reason to begin talking about your kids.) I mentioned that my son had just gotten his driver's license and said I wondered if I'd ever again get a good night's sleep, which explains why he volunteered that his own son had just survived a close call after an accident.

"John," he said, "I stood by his hospital bed for days, and

the only thing I could do was pray. Pray and pray and pray. I prayed until my soul bled."

Tears welled in his eyes, and his throat caught, so all he could get out was a weak, "But he's okay now. He's okay."

And that's when the bells at the church down the way began pealing.

God, what a moment.

I'm not a devoutly religious man, but I have never doubted the power of prayer, if only to clarify what someone wants or needs—or fears—at any given moment. Just as people who live alone often keep radios and televisions on in order to fill the emptiness, that voice in prayer, if nothing else, can help to make the world seem more intimate and less cold. A prayer is a declaration, silent or not, that implies someone is listening, maybe even sympathetically, and possibly with the power to take action.

It's said that there are no atheists in foxholes, which sounds right to me. But what are we to make of all the public prayer we see and hear these days, in places and situations that seem inappropriate to call God away from whatever else He's doing?

At sporting events, for example, players join clergymen in locker room huddles, then cross themselves at home plate and in the end zone; meanwhile, fans squeeze their hands together and beg God's favor during key moments—like fourth and long with less than a minute remaining. But it's not just big-event televised games at which people pray like they haven't since catechism (when they prayed to get out of there successfully). In my experience, seventh-grade soccer tournaments are just as full of prayer as the NFL.

At graduation ceremonies, speakers invoke the deity's blessing on behalf of those going forth.

In politics, prayers kick off inaugurations, congressional sessions, conventions, and breakfasts.

You even hear about the power of prayer when miners are rescued, accidents aren't fatal, and defendants are acquitted—guilty or not, by the way, like O. J. Simpson, Michael Jackson, and Robert Blake.

With there being 300 million Americans, on an ordinary day there might be as many as a billion prayers uttered—just in this country, which is less than 5 percent of the world's population. It's hard not to believe that, if God is indeed watching us and listening, He isn't a little annoyed by so many demands on His time. Common sense and logic—or at least a sincere respect for God—suggest that He has as much interest in the Super Bowl as He does in the Northeast Quadrant fantasy football pool. As for His stake in a recent graduate's success, seems to me that it's in direct proportion to how ambitious and determined that graduate is—while His guidance of politicians, no matter how genuinely they may pray to walk in His way, is probably less important to them than the latest polls.

What so many frivolous prayers represent, I think, is our struggle to understand how, if at all, God interacts with us in our lives. Myself, I have no idea, but I do have eyes and a brain, so I know that the most righteous of us are killed by bullets, falling pianos, and skidding gravel trucks—just as the least deserving of us frequently prosper unpunished. (A sure way to get a good conversation going is to ask your friends what they're most comfortable with: good things happening to bad people, or bad things happening to good people.)

I know that some of the most beautiful and innocent children meet unspeakable ends—just as the most heinously guilty often die safe and warm in their beds as old men.

I know that al-Qaeda credited Allah for bringing the destruction of Hurricane Katrina as a punishment for America's sins against Islam, and I also know that mere days later a powerful earthquake struck Pakistan and killed more than eighty thousand Muslims.

I know that the great tsunami of 2004 killed nearly two hundred thousand men, women, and children; and that Muslim imams blamed the devastation on the wickedness of women instead of on the failure of warning systems to clear the coastlines after a magnitude 9.15 undersea earthquake rocked the Indian Ocean.

I know that Pat Robertson blamed Israeli prime minister Ariel Sharon's cerebral hemorrhage on divine retribution for his abandoning Gaza to the Palestinians—"dividing God's land," Robertson said. But I also know that Sharon was a grossly overweight seventy-eight-year-old who got little exercise, ate mostly artery-clogging foods, endured constant stress—and lived nearly *twenty years past* what actuarial life expectancy was at the time of his birth.

These are facts, inconvenient as they may be, and for believers they tend to induce cognitive dissonance; I know that too. Any newspaper or news broadcast refutes the belief that God is a cosmic genie turning our infinite wishes into His commands, or that He rewards the pious for their faith with His favor. Torture and murder, disease and disaster afflict both the devout and the immoral every day. It has always been so.

And yet, every day people like my friend Victoria become atheists because life for them turned ugly. Losing both of her parents and her sister suddenly and unexpectedly within three months turned her from a believer to a cynical despiser. "I've lost my faith," she announced. "I don't believe in God anymore. God couldn't exist, or He wouldn't have let this happen. And if He does exist, and He let this happen, then . . ."

Why would she react that way? As an educated woman, Victoria had to recognize that as tragic as her losses are, history is written in the blood of innocents—tens of millions in just World War II alone.

The answer, it seems, is narcissism.

For a great example of how that kind of narcissism affects so many of us, and why it's so illogical, let's turn to a movie from a few years ago—*Signs*. Written and directed by M. Night Shyamalan, who's probably best known for *The Sixth Sense*, it starred Mel Gibson as a disgruntled minister. Well, maybe "disgruntled" doesn't do justice to his character's torment. Better to say that he'd lost his faith. And why? Because his wife had been hit and killed by a car.

Before telling you how this movie inadvertently dissects our narcissism so well, let me point out that it was a colossal success at the box office, earning nearly half a billion—that's *billion* with a "b"—dollars worldwide, more than half of that in this country, where it was said to be particularly popular with people of faith. And no wonder: it was well-made, well-acted, and utterly gripping—that is, if you didn't think too deeply about what you were seeing. Apparently, few did; maybe even none. Because in all the commentary about it, both professional and lay—critics and moviegoers alike—I never heard anyone else express the idea that the story was sheer, vainglorious poppycock.

Gibson's minister is from the beginning a man in agony, having already lost his wife. Of course, as a minister with a large flock in this pleasant town, many of his duties presumably included counseling the bereaved, those who'd lost parents and siblings and, yes, spouses—worse even, children—to fates far more painful and cruel than his wife's. Ah, but now that his own beloved had been taken from him, suddenly those platitudes and homilies he'd offered his congregants in their time of bereavement—no doubt believing his own words at the time—could not soothe his own grief; in fact, they seemed meaningless.

But here's the thing: his late wife had been *lated* not by a car careening out of control and jumping the sidewalk where she was walking to her next Meals-on-Wheels stop; not by a set of failed brakes sending the car through a wall and into the parlor where she sat knitting baseball caps for African AIDS orphans—but because she decided to walk late at night down a pitch-black country road wearing dark clothing. In other words, she was foolish, arrogant, and careless. Now, that's not the same as saying that she got what was coming to her. Neither, though, was her fate comparable to a child's fatal leukemia—and as a minister, Gibson's character should have known that. If he were going to lose his faith on account of unjust misery, he had plenty of reason to lose it long before then.

Wait, it gets worse. The action in the movie centers on an invasion of the earth by grotesque, murderous creatures. Though the camera never leaves the immediate area where Gibson and his remaining family live, viewers are shown via a television in the house broadcasting the news that tens of thousands, if not millions, of people are being savaged by the invaders. And yet, it's only when a Rube Goldberg–like series of events—at the time seemingly coincidental—lead to Gibson's son being saved from an alien that Gibson rediscovers God's goodness and grace, and his own faith. And what of all those other poor souls, not in the minister's orbit, who'd met hideous ends? Well, they must not have counted.

Hence, narcissism.

This minister, like my friend Victoria—like, no doubt, the majority of us—believes in God as a kind of servant, there to provide comfort and pleasure for me, me, me. And if He doesn't, then He's fired.

Hence, poppycock.

It doesn't serve believers, let alone the world, to believe that they're God's little buddies. But neither do intemperate remarks like Pat Robertson's about Ariel Sharon advance the message of mainstream Christianity. (Questions for Reverend Robertson: So God killed Ariel Sharon for giving away disputed land but let Hitler live long enough to cause the death of 50 million? Is that your position?) Nor do those imams' vicious comments about the tsunami's cause repair the tarnished reputation of Islam.

And thus we come to atheism—the idea that the universe was created by accident, that intelligence grew from no intelligence (talk about a leap of faith), that life's journey ends at death, and that deaf ears define the natural order.

Atheists scoff at prayer, because, they contend, there's no one to hear you anyway. Which, for all we can prove scientifically, may in fact be true. (Which is why we call it faith.)

But here's where it gets problematic for atheists (foxhole dwellers not included) who scoff: prayer works.

Prayer is a force of nature. Says who? Not me. Not Pat Robertson or Reverend Ike. Science says so, that's who.

On this, the medical literature is overwhelming. Study after study, hundreds of them, conducted under the kind of lab conditions that would survive the most withering defense attorney's cross-examination, have concluded that prayers can effect positive change in the human body. Though they may not win football games and elections—or if they can, it's not yet been proven—prayers can indeed heal the sick.

True, that's what the religion of Christian Science is founded on, but Christian Scientists are a preselected group predisposed to believe that prayer works and that their prayer group will help them beat cancer, heart disease, the flu, whatever. So to skeptics who insist on proof, their claims of having been healed may sound suspiciously like test patients who shout hallelujah over a migraine cured not by the powerful new drug they thought they were taking, but by a placebo.

Prayer, as it turns out, can work even if the patient doesn't do any of his own praying; even if he doesn't otherwise believe in the power of prayer; and, best of all, even if he doesn't know that he is being prayed for.

The most famous, if not the most comprehensive, scientific experiment on prayer was completed about twenty years ago at San Francisco General Hospital, out of the coronary care unit. It was a double-blind study on the therapeutic effects of what's called "intercessory prayer," conducted on nearly four hundred heart patients with great care taken to ensure that not only the patients themselves but also their families, their doctors, and other health care workers—in short, everyone but the computer who chose which patients would be in the test group and which in the control group—remained ignorant of the experiment. And none of the researchers knew which patient was in which group. Oh, and nothing was revealed about the patients' religious beliefs.

The study worked this way: People from afar were given

the first names only of patients to pray for (those in the test group) who had serious heart problems. For the remaining patients (those in the control group) no one prayed (aside from anyone in their own family who might be so inclined).

Across the board, the patients who received intercessory prayers from people they didn't know and didn't know were praying for them, required substantially less medication, developed far fewer complications, and were discharged earlier from the hospital than the control group.

Scientists and skeptics who've looked over the study, and literally hundreds like it, have found no methodological faults. But anyone who still finds cause for skepticism, believing that patients may somehow *subconsciously* react to the power of suggestion, should consider the more than one hundred studies conducted on nonhuman organisms. In his book *Healing Words*, a medical doctor named Larry Dossey reported that prayer helps yeast to better resist cyanide's toxicity, while lab rodents are aided in their fight against disease and grass grows taller when prayed over.

So what gives? It's a question the religious don't need to ask and the irreligious must answer.

Maybe prayer and a belief in God are not mutually exclusive concepts. That is, prayer may work not because God hears and answers, but because prayer is a force of nature—less understood for the moment than, say, gravity, but no less a part of the same scientific world that Newton began to describe when that apple fell on his head.

Think of radio waves filling the air. You can't see them, can't touch them, and can hear them only with a proper receiver. Well, what if the same could be said of prayer? What if the cosmos is a receiver that can transform thought waves into electrical impulses, which in turn act on a property the way that microwaves defrost chicken?

If my prayer-as-science hypothesis is correct, it shouldn't matter whether one kneels bedside to recite "Our Father who art in heaven . . ." or sits lotus-legged while chanting "Om." Prayer by any other name would sound as sweet to the laws of physics.

On the other hand, maybe it is indeed God's hand that makes some prayers come true. As my evangelical neighbor insists, God answers all our prayers; sometimes the answer is just plain no.

But for my new friend Ray at that factory, the answer was obviously yes. His son's recovery meant that his prayers had been answered, whether or not those prayers played any role. All things considered, it doesn't hurt to think they did and to act as though they do. The mind of man can never comprehend the complexities and mysteries, seen and unseen, of the world we live in, no matter who or what created it, and only a fool would pretend otherwise.

When those church bells stopped pealing, and the lump in my throat went down enough to speak, I didn't say a word. I just uttered a silent prayer of thanks—for him, for me, for all of us.

I REMEMBER LOVE SONGS

★　★　★

Warning: The following essay contains references to obscenities, and though I have obscured their spellings, they may offend some readers. Even so, I urge you to read anyway, because the topic is poison—not the kind that gets into your food and water, but the kind that gets into your soul and the souls of our children. We close our eyes and ears to it and pretend it's not there, at our own peril.

I have two children, a son and a daughter. When my son James was born, my first thought was about all the hunting and fishing and camping and sailing adventures we'd go on, and of how I'd show him the ropes of being a guy's guy. But two years later when my daughter Nina was born, my first thoughts were of protecting her from guy's guys.

Actually, that's only partly true. I also wanted to keep this beautiful girl from every kind of harm I could think of, not just future sixteen-year-old boys with groping hands and geyser testosterone. What I imagined for her when her time came was a young man with whom she could experience sweet romance: flowers, hand-holding, and tender kisses to the tune of "As Time Goes By."

Then I noticed something disturbing, courtesy of my nephew who was already approaching that less-than-tender age: "moonlight and love songs" had very much gone "out-of-date." We'd gone into a record store together to pick up a cassette he wanted, then popped it into the car's dash on the way home. What I heard was more revelation than music: it was 1990, and love songs bore little resemblance to the popular music that my generation and all previous generations had grown up with. Sad to say—and shocking—that they had essentially become audio porn.

Before, sex in music used to be couched in wonderful euphemisms that made them all the more romantic. The taboos of the time forced songwriters to create the feeling and excitement of sex without resorting to vulgarity, just as the so-called Hays Code that governed movies forced filmmakers to find creative and clever ways to convey the idea that a couple were going to be intimate with each other—a train entering a tunnel, for example, or curtains billowing at an open window.

Back when "love and marriage" went "together like a horse and carriage" and you weren't supposed to "sit under the apple tree with anyone else but me," song lyrics naturally equated the physical act with emotion. "Every time I look at you something is on my mind," went the lyric to "Sh-Boom" in 1954. "If you do what I want you to, baby, we'd be so fine."

Who among us figured out that the singers were talking about sex? And if we did, we sure didn't tell anyone else. Not till I hit adulthood did I understand the meaning of that "something" which was on the singer's mind—which was exactly the beauty of it, both literally and figuratively: a six-year-old, singing along with his mother in their '53 Chevy, didn't have to become prematurely initiated into an adult reality.

Unlike 1990. Having long before lost touch with popular music, not till then did I become aware that a kid riding along in his mother's '84 Dodge may have innocently turned on the radio to the local pop station and been exposed (kind of literally) to this song by N.W.A.: "Bitch, I'm gonna slap you upside the head with nine inches of"—never mind, you get the idea.

Then there was this 1987 song, "I Want Your Sex," by George Michael, who in those days was about the hottest act around: "Sex with me / Have sex with me / C-c-come on."

C-c-come on yourself, George.

Trust me, I'm not a prude. But I got incredibly angry at hearing that stuff go out over the airwaves, where in a few years my daughter's ears were going to be. I'd already made elaborate plans to keep her from the harms of certain television shows, never suspecting that radio was possibly more insidious—and far more available. I just hadn't noticed. Not until I had a daughter did I think about the issue for society. In some ways that makes me a cousin to Madonna, who, after a generation of polluting our children, decided a couple of years ago that her own children would be more or less kept under lock and key in a soundproof room, insulated from the harms of music like the kind she made.

No, I'm not as culpable as Madonna, because I didn't create any of that music. But neither did I support activist parent groups that had formed out of fear for the psychic health of kids exposed to such explicit lyrics—groups like the Parents' Music Resource Center, led by Tipper Gore, which, in the mid-1980s, began fighting to put warning stickers on albums that bear sexually explicit lyrics. Though I'm dubious about the worth of stickers—it seems to me they only call attention to the marked CDs and video games, like forbidden fruit—I would've liked to broaden the debate a bit and ask publicly: What good are warnings on merchandise if the same songs can be heard over the radio? Or, these days, through iPods? Now that the music doesn't necessarily blare through a car radio or stereo speakers, we parents sometimes don't have any idea what's going into our kids' ears and brains.

My fears then—as now—were not so much having my daughter's mind contaminated with filthy lyrics and therefore being inspired to rape, plunder, and pillage; parents, after all, are the source of their children's values and attitudes, not musical "artists." No, my fears were of her losing, way too soon, her innocence and healthy fantasies, and of desensitization, and most of all, of lowered romantic expectations. I didn't want her to think of sexual intercourse the way we used to think of kissing—as something you did, if you were lucky, on the third date. I wanted her to believe, when the time came, that sex is an expression of true love. And I didn't want her to mistake one for the other.

Even when I was sixteen and never more than four seconds from the next carnal thought, I remained at heart a romantic. I believed I had to have a relationship with a girl I was interested in and attracted to. And no wonder. All my life I'd been exposed to music (as well as movies, television, plays—the whole of popular Western culture) that couched humanity's rawest desires in, well, touching euphemisms (no pun intended). The language that formed my reference points had made physical contact somehow synonymous with, I guess you could say, spirituality.

"Tonight's the night I've waited for," Neil Sedaka announced.

"He kissed me in a way that I'd never been kissed before," cooed the Ronettes.

"In the still of the night, darling, I want to hold you so tight," sang the Five Satins.

"There is a rose in Spanish Harlem," Ben E. King told us about his secret love.

"Why do . . . lovers await the break of day?" asked Frankie Lymon and the Teenagers. (Hint: it's not for a cup of instant Folgers and the morning paper, though I didn't know that then.)

Even Buddy Holly couched his message. Consider "Not Fade Away" (covered a few years later by the Rolling Stones, the so-called "Bad Boys" of rock): "I'm gonna love you night and day . . ." (no longer a need to await the break of day).

★ My favorite euphemized lyric from back then comes courtesy of the Beatles: "She was just seventeen, and you know what I mean."

I'm happy that I'd already been exposed to all those thousands of innocuous love songs and movies before my libido awakened. I'm happy that, no matter how lasciviously those teenage hormones ran through me, I always related the idea of sex to love and romance. I'm happy not to have been cheated out of those thoughts. Because when I later began perceiving the hidden messages, I'd already had a lifetime's worth of romantic images to draw on. My fantasies of, chronologically, Simone Simon, Rita Hayworth, and Raquel Welch included some kind of relationship—at least meeting their parents—not just coupling. The same held true for other men I know who grew up in that musical climate. I can only conclude that women felt at least as romantic as we did, given that that's their nature anyway.

A twelve-year-old dancing in 1963 to "I Want to Hold Your Hand" managed quite nicely to miss that the song was about holding a lot more than the hand, just as to take someone's hand in marriage doesn't quite tell the whole story. But such innocent illusions are denied modern twelve-year-olds by the likes of Tone-Loc, whose top-ten hit "Wild Thing" when my daughter was a baby contained the line: "Couldn't get her off my jock / It was just like static cling."

Compare that with the hit song from the mid-'60s of the same name by the Troggs: "Come on and hold me tight / You move me." Remarkably, this used to be considered racy.

Compare the old standard "Fly Me to the Moon" (with the lyric "and let me play among the stars"), which is not so arguably about sexual pleasure, with the Black Eyed Peas recent song titled, appropriately enough, "Sexy," which urges to the object of the singer's desire, "Take off our clothes / We look better undressed."

Compare 1967's "Light My Fire" by the Doors—"Come on, baby, light my fire"—with Twista's "So Sexy" from 2004: "I gotta make her holla while I'm givin her dutty."

Compare the 1964 hit "(Just Like) Romeo & Juliet," which brags, "Take my girl cruisin' at the drive-in," with the Red Hot Chili Peppers' lyric "I want to party on your p----."

Compare the upshot of Little Richard's "The Girl Can't Help It"—"She make grandpa feel like twenty-one"—to Out-Kast's "Spread": "Can't resist your sexy ass / Just spread / Spread for me."

The examples are endless—on both sides.

If you're still reading and not retching—or purging your children's music collection, sledgehammering every radio in the house, and cross-checking every song on their iPods—try to remember that popular music isn't entirely a cesspool of unremitting derangement. The majority of songs today are probably as euphemized and falsely romantic as those of previous generations. So, as you maybe pay a little closer attention to your kids' listening habits than you might have been, take comfort in that.

But by the same token, be aware that it really only takes one song reveling in the graphic details to cheat young people out of even the illusion that Troy Donahue and Sandra Dee could join hearts by holding hands and kissing chastely. That's all it takes: a single song can blow the image that all generations were spared until about twenty years ago, when mores still demanded decorum. In 1956, for example, Little Richard reportedly was forced to change the second line in "Tutti Frutti" from "loose booty" to "Au Rutti." These days, "loose booty" would be a welcome relief compared to Ween's "Let Me Lick Your P----."

I doubt that any kid today who listens to the radio or watches MTV would misunderstand the meaning of the Stones' hit "Let's Spend the Night Together." Yet in 1966 I thought it was a nice song with a great backbeat. Where we were innocent, modern kids are "sophisticated," the very word a euphemism for having grown up too fast and too soon. It's easy to imagine dance floors of boys and girls screaming, in unison, "loose booty" at the appropriate place in the Little Richard song, their fists thrust into the air for punctuation, their faces bearing knowing smiles.

Of course, it's not just the music's fault. Through our divorce and murder rates, we've shown our children that neither love nor life is a certainty. Through our political processes, we've demonstrated that popularity—and doing anything to become popular—is of consuming importance. Through our general decline in standards, we've reduced their expectations to approach the lowest common denominator. Through our advertising, we've shown them that sex sells.

But of all possible factors in kids' lives, including parenting, music would seem to be up there among the most irresistible and influential. When my daughter was little and I was fired up about keeping her from harm, I found a study in the *Journal of the American Medical Association* stating that the average teenager listens to 10,500 hours of music between grades seven and twelve—just slightly less than the total number of hours he or she spends in the classroom from kindergarten through twelfth grade. And that was *before* iPods, which kids listen to everywhere all the time. That has to be a powerful influence even for those who aren't otherwise overly impressionable. I mean, how many times does a kid have to hear Keyshia Cole singing, "Let's go and get down and dirty" before he or she begins substituting images of condoms and motels for flowers and moonlight?

Oh, and let's not forget music videos. No matter how couched and euphemized a song's bump-thump content, the images will likely constitute a puerile sexual fantasy—like most of the videos I forced myself to watch back when my stomach was stronger and my blood pressure was lower. One of them stands out in memory: Billy Idol's video of "[Rock the] Cradle of Love" (a euphemism, I assumed, for what may be the singer's age preference). In it, a young girl walks into a man's apartment and performs an erotic striptease to the song she's inserted in his cassette player, thus unambiguously demonstrating what lies between the lyrics. So much for cutting to a train going into a tunnel. Of course, nowadays MTV is primarily a reality-show network, with shows in which young people "hook up" as easily as they used to hold hands at the malt shop. Which, come to think of it, is the logical outcome of everything they've seen and heard.

Years ago, rock and roll's rhythmic beat was enough to make a lot of adults think that it was the devil's music, because it supposedly led to sex. Now there's no question that it does. Now the songs leave so little to the imagination that even preteens can't miss that Christina Aguilera's dancing in "Dirrty" is mere foreplay: "I need that, uh, to get me off / Sweat'n 'til my clothes come off."

So the question now is whether it's possible for the average young person, attending a public school and raised by average parents (who are themselves products of the sexual revolution), to enjoy an old-fashioned romantic outlook. Or is sex to them now just little more than mutual masturbation?

Hoping for answers, I asked four neighborhood kids—two girls, two boys, ages fourteen, sixteen, seventeen, and eighteen—to tell me about their romantic expectations and whether they think things have changed over the years.

"People aren't looking for romance as much anymore. There's less than there used to be," said the eighteen-year-old, a boy.

"Human nature is the same; it's just gotten more complicated," said the seventeen-year-old girl.

"Things weren't as intense then," according to the fourteen-year-old girl.

"Yeah, I guess you could say we got a little bit cheated, you know, growing up fast," the sixteen-year-old boy lamented—or so I thought, until he added, "But I get a lot more than you did at my age."

Take that, old man.

Reeling, I called a high school biology teacher I know. Coincidentally, the semester before he had had an enlightening conversation about sex with his students. He asked them whether it was proper for thirteen- and fourteen-year-olds—that is, middle schoolers, their own younger brothers and sisters—to have sex. An overwhelming majority of the thirty kids agreed that it was entirely normal and proper—so long as they were in love.

Well, soon my daughter will be eighteen—and eligible to come out of her room for ten minutes a day.

THANK GOD IT'S WEDNESDAY

★   ★   ★

We usually clear out of a factory long before five o'clock, but on one particular summer day a big-rig accident on the Pennsylvania Turnpike tied up traffic, so we were late to arrive and late to leave—rushing the clock, in fact, before quitting time. My producer asked the shift manager whether some of the employees might be enticed to stick around for a while, in case we couldn't get done by five. "Probably not," the guy answered.

I could've told him that it was useless, having already talked to a worker whose big grin had fooled me at first sight. Walking by, I said, "You must love your job."

"I like it all right," he said.

"*Like* it?" I said. "You look happier than a mouse in the cheddar bin."

"Oh, sure," he said. "That's 'cause it's Friday."

As kids in school, most of us kept an eye on the clock and our minds on the calendar, eagerly anticipating that afternoon's three o'clock dismissal and then the two days of liberation brought by Fridays.

For most adults, apparently, not much has changed since then. Proclaiming it "happy hour," we stampede into bars at working day's end to refresh our sagging spirits with, well, spirits, and try to muster the courage and fortitude to make it to the fifth day. Then, throughout that fifth day, we're treated to the rallying cry, "Thank God it's Friday." There's even a major restaurant chain by that name, built on the supposition that Friday is the best day of the week because it means we don't have to work tomorrow or the day after.

But isn't there something inherently off with TGIF thinking? Doesn't it mean that we're wishing our lives away, or at least five-sevenths of it? Do the math for yourself. Anyone who expects to reach the age of eighty while simultaneously hoping for the weekend to hurry up and arrive is, in fact, mentally eliminating fifty-seven years of life.

How many of us, I wonder, would agree to a devil's bargain in which we exchange a long, bread-winning life, including weekends, for a leisurely one that ends at age twenty-three? Not many, that's for sure. And yet, we act that way when TGIF becomes our working mantra, even if it's said with a wink and a nod. That acronym is so embedded in the culture, it's as readily understood as FBI, CIA, and USA.

So what does that mean about us? That we hate our jobs or feel imprisoned by them? It sure seems so. And yet, the results of the last national poll I heard on the subject indicated that something like 70 percent of us enjoy at least a measure of job satisfaction. If the poll is to be believed—plus or minus the given margin of error—I suspect that more complex and insidious issues than simple job dread must be at work here. The disparity between what people tell Mr. Gallup and what they shout every Friday morning seems too great to be easily dismissed.

Wanting to know the answers to these great questions, I decided to play the role of intrepid investigator. As one who looks forward to his job and equally forward to being home with his family—and also somewhat uneasy over hanging out in a bar that's not a Hollywood set—I nonetheless dragged myself away one evening and took a seat at a saloon with a reputation for a decent happy-hour crowd. And you know what? I have to admit that the people there looked pretty happy. Maybe it was the two-buck well drinks and free leftover enchiladas.

Ambling incognito-ly around the circular bar, which was laden three deep in spots, I eavesdropped on snatches of conversation—you know, searching for behavioral clues. The ratio of let-me-show-you-my-etchings dialogue to authentic, end-of-the-day steam letting was about fifty-fifty. In fact, there didn't seem to be much said that fell between the two.

"I'd better go," groaned one woman dressed in a blue IBM-type business suit, after complaining about her supervisor for a full two minutes. "Gotta get some dinner and some sleep, so I can get up and do the whole thing all over tomorrow."

Nearby, a well-dressed man who'd kept punctuating his emphatic thoughts on each of the people in his office with "the bottom line" suddenly seemed to break character, if not context, by tilting back his head and roaring, "God, it sure feels good." Too bad I couldn't hear the punch line—the explanation for just *what* felt so good—before he brought his head forward and stared into his buddy's eyes.

"Know what I mean?" he asked.

"Yeah, I sure do," came the reply.

Well, I didn't.

I prayed that the guy in soiled blue overalls, drinking a beer across the way, might be offering some insightful information to the bartender, who seemed to be shirking his pouring duties in favor of attentive listening. By the time I got there, after stopping briefly to eavesdrop on a smooth operator—"You look exactly like Julia Roberts, I swear to God"—Mr. Overalls had gone. A few minutes later I saw him in the men's room. He was repairing an out-of-order urinal.

None of what I'd heard satisfied my curiosity. Either that or I didn't have the training to interpret the clues. Margaret Mead I'm not. So I called the closest person I know to that great anthropologist—a buddy who used to teach sociology in college. We met for lunch. I was early and he was late, so I had a few minutes to yak with the waitress and get her take on TGIF. She said she loved her job and all the people she meets, but by the same token she looked forward to getting off work every day— "and especially the weekends."

To be with friends and family, I assumed, projecting visions of a healthy, balanced life.

"Nope, I live alone," she said. "Look, I'll be honest. I love my job, but if I could get away with working a four-day or, even better, a three-day week, I'd do it in a heartbeat."

And if she could afford to retire?

"You kidding? I'd love it. I'd love never having to work again. That would make me very happy. Very, very, very happy."

By then my friend the ex-professor had shown up. He'd heard enough to launch into a long explanation about happiness being a relatively new concept, one born after the Industrial Revolution. He said that back when the endless days of

physical toil were interrupted only by a worshipful Sabbath—
which was spent in a stern religious institution that already governed daily behavior and morality—happiness was considered
a moment-by-moment proposition; it was not a permanent
emotional state to which one aspired. But as the advancing
technologies replaced manual labor, and people began working
jobs that required less time and physical effort, the pursuit of
chronic happiness began to seem like a reasonable and achiev-
able goal. Particularly since World War II.

"The sacred and the profane are almost reversed now," he
said. "Work has become sacred. It has a sense that 'this is the
core of my identity.' And though most people still consider
themselves religious, the weekend, which used to be a one-day
religious Sabbath, is now profane—two days to pursue the cult
of happiness. It's a cult of leisure, of sexuality, and of play."

That made sense to me. So did his explanation about how
Madison Avenue helps to shape our ideas of what to do in that
cult: buy what we see being offered by all those perfect-looking
women and men wearing perfect clothes and driving perfect
cars and having perfect fun. Those images breed a kind of advertising fantasy life, he said, and the closest most of us come to
feeling the way we assume those perfect creatures feel is at
night and on weekends. "That's what keeps people working:
they have to pay for their weekends."

"That sounds like psychology to me," I said.

"That's what advertising is," he said. "It's psychology."

And that, too, made sense. I figured I was really getting
close now to understanding how even people who love their
work still wish away five-sevenths of their lives. Believe me,
the competition in Hollywood is fierce, and those who brave
shark-infested moats and frequent humiliations so that they

can work on a film set twelve hours a day, at least five days a week, do it because they want it more than they want anything else in life—frequently including spouses, children, and security. Nearly everyone on a film set loves what they do and busted their buns to get the chance to do it. Yet, at the end of the work day, and most of all at the end of the week, you never saw people beat it out of there faster. The chants of TGIF—even if the "F" stands for Saturday or Sunday or whenever the last shoot day is—can be heard everywhere, including from the director and stars.

Which means, I think, that the psychological angle is the right one. Anyway, that's why I called a psychologist friend. At first he laughed when I asked him to shed some light on TGIF. Then he explained how, at least in America, the Protestant work ethic is still very much a part of the culture, even if the nature of our work has undergone revolutionary changes. "It's a vestige," he said, "but it's still there—and it's as emotionally severe as it always was."

"And that means what?" I asked.

"It means," he said, "that most workers believe, at least subconsciously, that work is hard and separate from their emotional needs, which are supposed to be met by family and friendships. So the dread comes not from the work itself, but from feeling stifled—which means that, at the end of the day, workers believe they have to anesthetize themselves with either drink or social contact or both. Hence, happy hour. Literally. That time becomes a sort of decompression chamber between the two distinct worlds, and weekends represent a 'brief respite of self-integration.'"

"What about Thursday?" I asked.

"What about it?" he said.

I told him that I'd heard Thursdays were becoming the busiest night out for restaurants and theaters, rivaling Fridays and Saturdays.

"And your point is?" he said.

My point was that Thursday signifies that "Miserable Monday" seems much further away on Thursday than it does on Friday; it's the distant future, not the second day after tomorrow, as it would be if today were Friday, or the day after tomorrow on Saturdays, or, worst of all, tomorrow if this were Sunday. So, Thursday night brings the highest sense of anticipation, which for most of us may be as close to the moment of enjoyment as we get. After all, once the moment is with us, by definition it's gone. Sure, vacations are wonderful, but once they've begun, every day that passes brings them closer to their end. Our sense of excitement, it seems, is never as high as when we're packing to go. (Old joke: "How was your vacation, Al?" "I don't know. I haven't gotten my pictures developed yet.")

A long time ago, in a galaxy far, far away called the 1960s, I attended a lecture by one Baba Ram Dass (née Richard Alpert), the former Harvard researcher whose repeated LSD experiments propelled him on some sort of quest that culminated in his becoming a Hindu. He had just written a book, *Be Here Now*, about the difficulty Westerners have remaining focused in the moment. Only physical pain or pleasure, bringing us to a heightened awareness of *now*, he said, are easy antidotes for the steadily flowing subconscious river that ferries us from the past to the future, and back again, without stopping for long in the middle.

I understood completely what he was talking about. The day before the lecture I'd attended a Rolling Stones concert, for which I'd previously slept on the street to buy tickets and, in frenetic anticipation, had marked off the days on a calendar. My greatest thrill of the afternoon was when the announcer said, "Ladies and gentlemen, the Rolling Stones!" After that, it was all downhill.

"So what are you doing tonight?" I asked the worker at the factory on that Friday. "Big plans, huh?"

"Naw," he said. "Nothing special. But tomorrow— tomorrow's my boy's first birthday."

Now *that's* a worthy TGIF.

ONE NATION

★　★　★

One of the hardest parts about doing *John Ratzenberger's Made in America* is all the travel—tens of thousands of miles a season. And one of the best parts about doing the show is all the travel—which puts me in contact with people I would've never met otherwise, ordinary people doing extraordinary things. People like Reverend Carl Hardin, in Jefferson City, Missouri.

We were on our way to the Everlast plant in Moberly, where boxing gear is made, and found ourselves in a poor part of the state's capital, driving past houses that had seen better years and cars that may not even have been drivable. Looking out the window I happened to notice a large man teaching some small kids how to box. The sight was compelling enough. And then I noticed that the tattered lawn on which they were practicing their jabs belonged to a Baptist church. I asked the driver to stop and got out to look around.

That large man turned out to be Reverend Carl, pastor of the church and coach of its boxing club, which is intended, of course, to keep kids off the street and out of trouble. Boxing,

244 ★ WE'VE GOT IT MADE IN AMERICA

the good reverend explained to me, develops self-confidence of the type that lets young men whose veins are raging with testosterone believe that they don't have to prove anything to anyone in more violent and less productive ways.

He took me inside the building and showed me proudly where they worked out, and all I could think about was what these poor (literally) people didn't have—everything, basically. They shared a single pair of gloves, were missing a ring, and had to take turns practicing on a heavy bag, tied to a tree branch, that looked like it had spent the last twenty years alternating between the microwave and freezer. Which it had, in a way, given the Missouri winters and summers. All things considered, they might as well have been a football team without a football.

I didn't tell Carl where we were on our way to (though it sure seemed divinely provident) and he didn't ask; he was glad to take us around, even if the only reason we showed up was to feed our curiosity. "Was good to see you," he said as we left.

But when we made it to the Everlast plant the next day, Reverend Carl and his church's boxing team was all I wanted to talk about with the plant manager, Ray Stuart. Well, you know what Ray did? God bless him, he showed up at the church with us that evening and surprised Reverend Carl and his young people with boxes and crates and, yes, a ring—a boxing ring—full of everything a legitimate boxing team needs to get its hopefuls to the Olympics, or at least off the streets. All of it donated by Everlast.

You should've seen those kids. If you had, you would never ever doubt how rich you feel when you give. Probably for the first time in their lives, these kids had caught a real break. They were animated and giddy, trying everything with the joy of

Christmas morning. The adults hugged each other and us. Prayers of praise and gratitude increased the happiness, and everyone knew that this small bit of good fortune was a first step to—well, that was up to the kids. But now they knew that miracles can and do happen when you ready yourself for them.

As we left, I felt exhilarated—and was instantly reminded of something remarkable that had happened to me a few years before.

I was in Kinsale, a picturesque village on the southwest Irish coast, with actor Barry Lynch, walking through the narrow cobblestone streets. Hungry and not knowing that the town was famous for its food, we ducked into the first restaurant we saw, which just happened to be Chinese—owned by a man straight off the boat from Qingdao. It was mid-afternoon, so we had the restaurant to ourselves and took a booth by the window.

As soon as we sat down I noticed a group of ten girls, probably eight to twelve years old, dressed in their school uniforms, walking by. Idly, they looked in, saw Barry, did a double take, chattered excitedly, and kept walking. We laughed. Barry's a handsome man, and apparently in Ireland he's as well-known as Pierce Brosnan is here.

The street door clanged open, and I glanced up. It wasn't another hungry mu shu pork fan. It was the schoolgirls, filing in. The oldest led the way to our table, holding a large portfolio with some papers peeking out that looked like sheet music.

"Are you Barry Lynch?" she asked.

"I am," he said.

"Oh," she said, as the others smothered their giggles, "may we have your autograph?"

"Of course," he said, and as he was signing she looked up at me. Her eyes widened in recognition and surprise.

"And aren't you the one from *Cheers*?" she asked.

"Yes, I am," I said, and she turned back excitedly to the other girls, then back to me.

"Can we be getting your autograph as well?" she asked.

"It would be my pleasure," I said, taking the pen. "Now it's my turn to ask *you* a question. What's that in your hand?"

"It's our music," she said. "We're the choir for St. Agnes Church."

"Well now," I said. "Are you just coming from rehearsal?"

"Yes, we're on our way home."

"And what have you been rehearsing?"

"The *Ave*," she said.

"The *Ave*? That's my absolute favorite song ever," I said. "Would you mind singing it for us?"

"Right now?"

"Yes, why not?"

She glanced back at her choir mates and they did some fast talking with their eyes before she turned my way and nodded, "All right."

Now they moved quickly into formation. The leader breathed deep and sounded the first note, and at that they began what was, is, and will forever be the most beautiful *Ave Maria* of my life. A perfect harmony of voices filled with an innocence and purity that could make you believe the mother of God was there in the room.

Tears filled my eyes as they sang, and when Barry and I applauded, I heard another pair of hands—the restaurant owner's, standing by the kitchen door. The man barely spoke English and was likely not a Catholic, but just the same the tears had been streaming steadily out of his eyes.

The girls bowed, we thanked them, and they left. Through

the windows, we watched them walking until they were out of sight. I found myself hoping that they had some understanding of the gift they'd just given us.

Now, I didn't tell you these two stories in order to give Ray Stuart and Everlast and Reverend Carl another pat on the back, though Lord knows they all deserve one; nor am I inclined to brag gratuitously about one of my most memorable experiences. No, I related these stories because, together, they're bookend symbols of something that this country, for all its affluence, is losing—the heart of what makes America great from the inside out. And because of that, we may be paying a price beyond what any of us can bear: the future.

Let me explain, to see if you think I'm being overly dramatic.

What I first noticed about the Irish schoolgirls was that they were outside, walking. And curious about someone they thought they recognized, they were brave enough to investigate, even if it meant wandering into a place of business where they weren't going to spend a dime. That's a lot, especially given their ages.

These days, in this country, most young people seem poisonously timid about strangers, no doubt because they've been taught not to speak to them by parents who apparently believe that bad guys with evil intentions are lurking around every corner. Not long ago I saw a kid on his bike drop a school book, but when I shouted to him about it, he kept riding, fearful that it was a trick. The book lay there until I picked it up and returned it to the school named on the inside.

Thanks to the news media, I suppose you can't fault parents for teaching their kids caution—anyway, I won't fault them—no matter that the hysteria about kidnappings by strangers isn't supported by facts and figures; kids are not disappearing at higher rates than they were four decades ago. Even so, and even if the boogeyman does exist, I know instinctively that insulating children in a parental cocoon, where they can't develop their own interior bs detectors, harms them more than helps them.

And that's the context that made the encounter with the church choir so emotionally satisfying: I knew as it was happening that the streets I walk in America offer little or no chance of a shared impromptu experience to compare—something that surprises and delights, and connects us as Americans. The closest I've come since was that morning in Missouri.

What first caught my eye while driving past that church was not the neighborhood's poverty, because stricken neighborhoods are in every city and town, including and especially where I grew up. It was that there were actually kids outside, doing what kids are supposed to do on pleasant summer days. Where I travel, most kids don't seem to do that much anymore—not spontaneously, anyway. Which exactly explains the problem.

When I was a kid, a dry sky and temperatures above fifty pretty much guaranteed that every park in town would be full of kids playing ball, or just fooling around. It didn't matter how many of us there were, we'd concoct a game right on the spot to accommodate either too many or too few bodies for any of the regular rules. Football, baseball, basketball, kickball, stickball, over the line, whatever—the list was endless, including names long forgotten and games that only had a name for that one day only. (One kid and I would sometimes meet early in the morning at elementary school, long before the PE director or anyone else was there, and play dodgeball in front of the handball wall with my sweater that we'd rolled and tied into a round shape.)

And because we had to pick captains and stand there as

they chose sides every time, there was always a moment of pride or despair—or something in between—while you waited to be chosen. Some were always chosen first and some usually last, and even if you were in the latter group you still stood there with the hope of proving and improving yourself, and therefore rising in the hierarchy for the next time. My sense is that we all learned as much about life and each other and disappointment and grace and self-esteem and how to handle a lack of it—in other words, what takes place in *real* life—than we did from almost anything else. We built self-esteem by earning it, and we learned to handle not being as good as some others without complaining to our dads about how unfair life is (not that they would've commiserated anyway). We either did something about our lot by working harder, or we sucked it up and did what we could anyway.

These days, the only kids I see playing in parks—if I see them at all—are wearing team uniforms. And of course, unlike me and the kids I grew up with—and the kids I saw at the Baptist church—they're all middle-class or upper-middle-class. They play in organized leagues, and have scheduled games— which we did, too, of course, but that was only dessert for us; the main course was just being out there to fool around and knock heads.

Kids wearing uniforms are already part of an established team—soccer, baseball, whatever—so they know every day whom they're going to be playing with and against. Other than making the team, they don't suffer any rites of passage; if they can't excel at one game, they or their parents move them to another. And because coaches lead them through practice drills, they don't have a chance to develop much spontaneity, or even creativity. My guess is that if you took five of these kids at random, put them on an empty grass field without adult supervision, and gave them something soft and round—like a rolled-up sweater—they'd be at a loss to come up with anything fun, and would probably decide to go inside and play video games or watch some tube.

After practice, the kids are picked up by their parents and driven somewhere else, probably home, maybe piano lessons, maybe karate, maybe another sport. Their lives are segmented, regimented, and directed. They don't play anymore. They have "playdates"—arranged and scheduled by their parents. And that's not good news. The message we inadvertently give them is that life is a sequential series of entertainments—like a night of television, one program after another. Scripted, too. That doesn't do them any favors or help prepare them for life outside Mom and Dad's embrace.

And what an embrace it is. It's an embrace born of love, yes, but mostly of fear—fear that Junior or Missy won't be successful as we now define the term: rich. It's an embrace meant to instill life into them by shielding them from real life.

Remember that Massachusetts father who beat another father to death over their sons' hockey game? Or the Pittsburgh T-ball coach who promised one of his seven-year-olds twenty-five dollars to bean another of his lesser players—a boy who was mildly autistic and therefore not very good—so that he wouldn't have to play him in an "important game"? The manslaughtering father believed that his son's hockey game was the most important thing in the world, and the soliciting coach believed that there was such a thing as an important T-ball game. You should know, too, that when the bean ball didn't hurt the kid sufficiently, the other boy threw another ball into his groin. Wait, it gets worse still: the mother of the injured boy—who ended up in the hospital—only went to the police when the league refused to act on her complaint about the coach's offer.

I wouldn't be surprised to hear that there may be hundreds of stories around the country of criminal sideline rage similar to these, even if they don't make the news. For years I've watched my children and the children of my friends play organized sports and been appalled by the behavior of parents for whom sportsmanship seems to be an obsolete notion. No, that's too kind, too understated. Better to say that they've studied ethics under Tonya Harding, the ice-skater who paid two men to kneecap her Olympic rival Nancy Kerrigan—or the Texas cheerleader's mom who plotted to murder the mother of her daughter's rival, reasoning that the rival would be too distraught to cheerlead.

I remember watching the twelve-year-old daughter of my good buddy play soccer in the first round of her league's regional playoffs against a team that had clearly been coached to throw elbows and trip faster girls when they flew by—like my friend's daughter, an incredibly fast runner who was sent flying by an intentional trip that kept her from scoring and almost sent her to the hospital. The whole game went like that, with "our" girls getting hammered as the opposing parents screamed obscene encouragement to their girls and, when our girls got near their sideline or had to throw the ball in from that side, taunted them with vulgarisms and threats. Of course, that was all of a piece with what had happened before the game, when the opposing coach and two of his larger girls waited on the sidelines for our girls and snarled menacingly, "We've been waiting to kick your butts!" Then, having lost, the losers spit in their hands after the game to contaminate their high fives for what's supposed to be the "Hey, nice game" moment.

I also remember seeing eleven-year-olds playing basketball

against a team that had been coached to pull down the pants of our boys as they shot, an act for which they received at most a simple foul. The other parents laughed each time, as did the coach. One mother on our side told me that her younger son had just lost a game the previous day 66-2. "Three minutes left," she said. "It was fifty-six to two, and a parent on the other side was screaming bloody murder at the ref for calling traveling on his son, his face all red like he was going to burst. And he's ahead by fifty points. You wouldn't have believed it."

I believe it. And I believe that you don't need Nostradamus to foresee what kinds of adults these kids are going to grow up to be.

But from my vantage, the issue is larger than boorish behavior in adults and future adults who then pass on their values to the following generation; that's only one part of the problem, and it's a symbol of something even more worrisome and dreadful.

The issue is that we're creating a world for our children that is beginning to look more like Mad Max's Thunderdome than the America built on American dreams. Put another way, it feels like a violent game of musical chairs with the players believing that the consequences of not finding a seat are too terrible to contemplate, so they resort to the law of the jungle in order to survive.

Fewer and fewer of our children are having fewer and fewer shared experiences that aren't preplanned. Those kids in their uniforms aren't playing Little League as part of their ordinary summer. They're being taught to win, not to play. They likely attend special summer camps to hone their baseball or soccer or volleyball skills, and they belong to teams that are scouted by college coaches with scholarships to hand out to the best.

They're learning from their parents that it's not how you win but that you *do* win. Any way you can. Period.

We give them music gizmos that they wear when they're alone, which means that even on the street they feel separate and apart, self-absorbed in the soundtrack of whatever movie they're living as protagonist. And when they're with their friends, feeling emboldened by numbers, they're either unaware of or indifferent to the fact that a public space ought to have some rules—as in, keeping your voice respectably low, and not uttering vulgarisms where others might hear. Don't bother pointing that out to them, either, or asking them to curb their language on the grounds, say, that you're with your mother or daughter or wife—that is, unless you're itching for a fight.

"What're you?" they'll say indignantly. "A cop?" Or, "You're not my father, you can't tell me what to do."

The truth, though, is that they're really only emulating what they consider to be adult behavior. More or less, it's what they see us do. We drive as though we think we're the only car on the road, taking it as a hanging offense when another car has the temerity to get in our lane ("Cover me, honey, I'm gonna pass the Ford").

We talk on cell phones in public as though we were encased in an invisible glass phone booth, oblivious that we may be infringing on others. Restaurants, streets, museums, trains, movie theaters—no place is safe from cell breach. I remember the man in an airport terminal talking so loudly on his cell that everyone for four gates could glean the details of the big deal he was working on. Finally I walked over and stood next to him, repeating everything he'd just said but even louder through cupped hands, pretending it was for the benefit of anyone who might be hard of hearing—or sitting next to the television blaring CNN.

"Hey, this is a private conversation," he barked.

"And that, sir, is a telephone, not a megaphone," I said, to applause.

And let's not forget how we dress in public: as though we'd just come from clearing out the garage—jeans, flip-flops, T-shirts—no matter where we're going. It's nothing anymore to see old jeans and untucked shirts at the fanciest restaurants in town. Or when addressing City Hall, touring the White House, visiting business offices. I've seen adult men wearing shorts at Broadway shows, where performers dedicate their lives to the art and craft of exquisite entertainment—and yet these guys show up looking like they're back from the 7-Eleven after a large Slurpee, plastic bags and all. I've even seen them dressed like that at funerals. To them, nothing's sacred, everything's profane, and no stranger deserves the respect that comes with presenting well.

In short, we have degraded the whole idea of shared space, turning the exterior world into an extension of our living rooms. No wonder our kids have little sense of decorum and take such offense when you point it out to them. They consider propriety an invasion of their rights—as in, "I have a right to do whatever I want."

Meanwhile, the failures of our public education system are turning out two distinct classes of young people. In the first are those who (presumably like Reverend Hardin's boxers) are going to find it very difficult, even assuming they complete high school, to compete against the other class of young people—which is an increasingly large class: those who abandon public education and matriculate through private schools. Why? Because it's likely that private-school kids will know more by the time they finish high school than the other kids ever do. Yes, some will catch up—and even surpass their more privileged peers. But the great majority won't. And the growing divide between the two creates an unsustainable, third-world society, with implications far beyond how well Johnny or Judy do individually.

At a Christmas gathering last year, I was showing some teenagers how to play bocce ball in the backyard of my buddy's house. Two of them, a twelfth-grade boy attending public school and a ninth grader from a private school, had to wait their turn and got into a discussion about teachers. The older boy was complaining about having to read so many books for his English class. The younger boy asked what they were, and the older boy named the three novels from the previous semester: *The Great Gatsby, Heart of Darkness*, and *The Catcher in the Rye*.

"Oh," said the younger boy, "they're all pretty short."

"How do you know?" the older boy asked, obviously surprised that the younger kid would be familiar with the titles.

"Well, we did *Gatsby* last month, along with *The Sun Also Rises* and *The Sound and the Fury*. That was a little hard to understand, but it was pretty good. Let's see, *Catcher in the Rye* was, I think, uh, seventh grade. Good book. Fun. I liked Holden Caulfield, but I liked his sister Phoebe better. Oh, and *Heart of Darkness*, I'm reading that now; that's just for over the holidays. You think there's going to be a lot more action in it, but I guess that's what was considered pretty harsh for its time. After we get back I think she's got *Gone with the Wind*, which is kinda thick, so we'll probably get a whole month. Tenth grade's the real hard-ass: two or three Russian novels the first semester. I hear the AP classes really pile it on."

For all his education, the younger boy had no clue what messages he'd been giving the older boy, whose face looked like it was caught in the teeth of invisible vise grips.

"What colleges did you apply to?" the younger boy asked.

The answer was state colleges, which are perfectly fine institutions, especially in this state. But I could tell that, to the younger boy, the term "state college" had about the same connotation as "state prison."

For me, there was a whole universe of meaning in that moment.

Later, I sought out the older boy's father and managed to work the conversation gently in a direction that would tell me even more than I'd already heard. He was a man of modest means whose son was a good boy who did what he was told and got decent grades. He followed the rules, expecting them to pay off. But he never even considered an elite college, not because he doesn't have the capability of succeeding in one, but because he'd spent his childhood years growing up, not burnishing his credentials or resumé. Nonetheless, he's the type of kid who'll do just fine in life. But he and the ninth grader will reside in separate Americas, having little real connection outside of whatever incidental contact there may be in the workplace.

Talking to him, I couldn't help thinking of Reverend Hardin's grateful boxers—kids who'd think that they'd won the lottery to have even ordinary opportunities. And I thought of the girls' choir in Ireland, free on the street, walking, cautious but fearless, engaged, involved, curious, their *Ave Maria* transforming the ordinary into the extraordinary.

I thought of the boy on his bike, refusing to come back for his dropped book; and of the ballplayers in uniforms going through their drills before being picked up; and of me and my buds, waiting to be chosen for touch football; and of the red-faced parents shouting on the sidelines.

And soon all those thoughts jumbled together into a fog that blotted out other thoughts, even of the holiday. Fear rose in their place. I felt afraid—afraid of the gulf that divides us and that seems to be growing wider. I took that fear to bed with me that night and slept fitfully, worried for our future. For the future of my children's country.

When I woke the fear was still with me, so I went out for jog, but I could not sweat out the fear nor run from it. Back at home, wondering if I were going a little bit mad, I switched on the radio and heard one of the speakers interviewing a September 11 widow who was spending another Christmas alone. And then I remembered how, in the midst of all that grief and anger, we had come together as one—Americans all, black and white and brown and yellow, rich and poor and middle-class, young and old, landed and immigrant. And that broke the fear. Because underneath it all, we really are one country. Sure, in the best of times—uneventful times—maybe we act like siblings who can barely tolerate each other and compete to see who Dad loves more. But when something happens, the blood thickens real fast. And that's what counts. And that's what will always, always, always bridge all the great divides between us.

CREDITS

★

Authors . . . . John Ratzenberger
. . . . Joel Engel
Editor . . . . Christina Boys
Assistant Editor . . . . Meredith Pharaoh
Publisher . . . . Rolf Zettersten
Publisher's Assistant . . . . Kathie Johnson
Associate Publisher . . . . Chip MacGregor
Associate Publisher's Assistant . . . . Heidi Nobles
Managing Editor . . . . Harvey-Jane Kowal
Production Manager . . . . Dylan Hoke
Production Associate . . . . Nikki Cutler
Production Assistant . . . . Grace Hernandez
Production Editor . . . . David Palmer
Copy Editor . . . . Karyn Slutsky
Designer . . . . Victoria Hartman
Proofreaders . . . . Jill Amack
. . . . John Vasile
Cover Design . . . . Jody Waldrup
Cover Photographer . . . . Dean Dixon
Cover Copy Coordinator . . . . Holly Halverson
Cover Production Director . . . . Antoinette Marotta

Book Typeset by Stratford Publishing Services
Book printed by Quebecor World
Cover printed by Jaguar Advanced Graphics